D1241010

★ OUR ★ THREATENED FREEDOM

A Christian View on the Menace of American Statism

ROUSAS JOHN RUSHDOONY

VALLECITO, CALIFORNIA

Copyright 2014
Mark R. Rushdoony

Chalcedon/Ross House Books
PO Box 158
Vallecito, CA 95251

www.ChalcedonStore.com

All rights reserved.

No part of this book may be reproduced, stored in a retrieval system, or transmitted in any form or by any means — electronic, mechanical, photocopy, recording, or otherwise — except for brief quotations for the purpose of review or comment, without the prior written permission of the publisher.

Library of Congress Catalog Card Number: 2014943960
ISBN: 978-1-879998-70-4

OTHER TITLES BY ROUSAS JOHN RUSHDOONY

The Institutes of Biblical Law (3 volumes)
Systematic Theology (2 volumes)
Commentaries on the Pentateuch:
Genesis, Exodus, Leviticus, Numbers, Deuteronomy
Chariots of Prophetic Fire
The Gospel of John
Romans & Galatians
Hebrews, James & Jude
The Cure of Souls
Sovereignty
The Death of Meaning
Noble Savages
Larceny in the Heart
To Be As God
The Biblical Philosophy of History
The Mythology of Science
Thy Kingdom Come
Foundations of Social Order
This Independent Republic
The Nature of the American System
The "Atheism" of the Early Church
The Messianic Character of American Education
The Philosophy of the Christian Curriculum
Christianity and the State
Salvation and Godly Rule
God's Plan for Victory
Politics of Guilt and Pity
Roots of Reconstruction
The One and the Many
Revolt Against Maturity
By What Standard?
Law & Liberty
A Word in Season series

CONTENTS

SERIES ONE

SERIES TWO

SERIES THREE

SERIES FOUR

SERIES FIVE

SERIES SIX

SERIES SEVEN

SERIES EIGHT

SERIES NINE

SERIES TEN

SERIES ELEVEN

SERIES TWELVE

SERIES THIRTEEN

FOREWORD

THE COLLECTION OF 155 essays in this volume was originally recorded as radio spots between 1980 and 1983 by my father, R. J. Rushdoony. Details of where they were originally broadcast and the individuals who were responsible have been lost with the passing of time. The texts were found in my father's papers, but the sound recordings might have been lost if it were not for Rev. Byron Snapp of Calvary Reformed Presbyterian Church in Hampton, Virginia. He and his wife Janey were original sponsors of their broadcast in South Carolina and still had cassettes of the original recordings. He graciously offered them to Chalcedon in 2005. Since then, they have been used as podcasts by Chalcedon and some of the texts have also been published on *www.chalcedon.edu* and elsewhere. This is the first time they have been published as a collection. There were originally 169 spots, but a few were deemed to be too dated to contemporary events to warrant publication.

My father was a keen observer of cultural trends and had the resolve and capacity to view all things through a Biblical lens. The topics he addressed were decidedly relevant to his audience when originally broadcast and continue to be thematically relevant into the twenty-first century. My father saw the outcomes of humanistic thinking and the policies and programs that would logically flow from them. More importantly, though, he was ready and able to posit the remedy. He did not merely act as the harbinger of "bad news," but served as the herald for truly Biblical solutions.

Though some of the specific news events, court cases, or legislation on which he commented are no longer current, he provided us with a mature example of a covenantal, ethical, and judicial examination of current events. His comments are pastoral and theological, not political. Unlike many popular news sources today, he did not put a spin on the news to advance a particular political goal or agenda. His did not mold his message around a conservative Republican agenda—he wrote and spoke as a man who feared God, who saw all of life through the lens of God's enscriptured Word, and who had a fervent desire to know how God's Word was applicable to our times.

My father wrote again and again against statism and the pervasive confidence, common to both the left and the right, in political salvation. Whether propounded by those who claim to be liberal or conservative, the end result of that approach is always the empowerment of the state and hence the loss of liberty. Man is saved not by legislation, elections, or politics, but by Jesus Christ; and the fundamental level of government is the self-government of the Christian man before God. Only this represents a real liberty. The security of the state is a fraud, a counterfeit of true freedom which produces dependence on the least productive or progressive aspect of a culture. In these bite-sized, easily-digestible essays, my father gives exposés of both the domination and tyranny of the modern state as well as its pathetic incompetence in trying to supplant the Kingdom of God. The importance of self-government is shown implicitly by contrasting it with the ugly alternative. Freedom is not ultimate in Biblical thought, but it is a necessary element in the fulfillment of our Christian duties. Liberty's greatest blessing in the Christian perspective is its enablement of the believer's service in his primary citizenship, that of the Kingdom of God. A slave serves his master. As free men we are called to use our liberty in the service of our God and His Christ.

It is my hope that these brief essays will encourage you in your faith, and serve as a reminder of the great need to think Biblically in all areas of life as you work to exercise dominion in His name.

Mark R. Rushdoony

★ SERIES ONE ★

★ *one* ★

IS THE CHURCH A CHARITABLE TRUST?

THE FIRST AMENDMENT, with its assurances of freedom and religion, the press, and more, is steadily being eroded, and new doctrines of statist control are replacing it.

Our concern today is with one aspect of this charge, as it affects religious liberty. Various federal agencies, and many states, are quietly reclassifying the church, the Christian school, missionary agencies, monastic orders, and the like as charitable trusts. At first glance, this seems to make no appreciable difference; the tax-exempt status continues, and there is no dramatic change. A charitable trust, however, is an organization which is accountable to the state for the use of its funds and properties without regard to race, color, or *creed*. That last is the critical point.

If a church must represent all creeds and religions, it ceases to be a church. A charitable trust is by law under state control. United Way is a classic example. To reclassify churches as charitable trusts is to make them state churches. It means also that, whenever civil authorities choose to do so, they can require that a church give equal time to all religions. A Buddhist temple (and there are a few in the United States) would have to give equal time to Christianity and Mohammedanism, and likewise the various Christian churches would have to give equal time to all other religions.

Somewhere down the road, this will be required of our churches unless changes are made soon. In at least one case, in California, the state argument against a church was that, "The Court is the ultimate custodian of all church funds . . . The institution itself and all of those who run the institution are standing in a position of trust, the property being truly owned, not by the institution or individuals, but rather the people of California . . . Under [the laws of the State of California], although the property is held by the charitable organization, it is held for the benefit of the public at large."

In other words, your church does not belong to you: it belongs to the state, and it can be taken from you at the will of the state. Let me add that this situation is not unique to California, but is common to most of the country.

But the church is not a charitable trust, nor is it state property. The whole point of the First Amendment is to preserve religion from state controls. The church belongs to God. It is responsible to Christ and to the people who support the church. The attempt of bureaucrats to call the church and its agencies charitable trusts has an obvious motive: to place the church under state controls and to give it the same blessings of mismanagement which they give to everything else.

The issue is one of control. Should the state, or the Internal Revenue Service, or some other agency control the church? Who is Lord over the church—Christ or Caesar?

Do we still regard the First Amendment as a part of the Constitution? The First Amendment was adopted because the clergy of all the states demanded it. They were afraid of a federally controlled or established church, and with good reason. Last year, at the demands of countless Americans, Congress adopted the Ashbrook and Dornan Amendments. These tied the hands of the IRS for the fiscal year, barring it from intervening in the affairs of Christian schools and churches. Now the IRS seeks freedom from such restraints for the coming fiscal year.

Unless we stand for freedom, we will soon have nothing to stand for.

★ *two* ★

FREEDOM OR CONTROLS?

FREEDOM OF SPEECH and of press are set forth in the First Amendment. In recent years, we have seen serious limitations placed on those freedoms by the courts. The courts have, in some decisions, seriously limited the press and its freedom. Radio and television are extensively controlled by the federal government. In some states, securities commissions require all economic newsletters published in those states to be licensed.

Now, we can argue with more than a little evidence that the press is often irresponsible and gives one-sided reporting. Most of us can recall very telling examples of this. We should remember, however, that the framers of the Constitution and the Bill of Rights were well aware of this. Some of the newspapers of their day were worse than anything we can imagine. When George Washington was president, for example, some newspapers went far beyond all decency in attacking him. One especially vicious editor was Benjamin Franklin Bache, grandson of Benjamin Franklin.

Bache claimed that the humble Washington behaved "with all the insolence of an Emperor of Rome." Among other things, Bache published a long attack by Thomas Paine on George Washington. Paine accused Washington of everything from fraud to murder, hypocrisy, and worse. Paine was an unbeliever; Washington fasted every Sunday and was a devout man. Nevertheless, Paine accused him of apostasy, and Bache published this and more.

Now, the important fact is that neither Washington nor his administration moved to limit the freedom of the press. Why?

The reason is simple. Any law passed is easily circumvented by the lawless. The end result of every restrictive law, whether control of the press or gun control, is that it will control the law-abiding, not the lawless. The law-abiding are always the most easily controlled, because all their activities are open and aboveboard. This is not all. Every law passed ends up meaning far more than the framers intend, because the courts place interpretations on every word that stretch the boundaries of the law and increase the powers of the state.

But there is more to this. A controlled communications media and a controlled press only limit the freedom of responsible agencies. The irresponsible agencies are rarely affected; they never invest too much capital in any single operation and can easily shut down one operation to begin another.

We may with good reason dislike much that exists in the press and all the communications media. However, if we limit their freedom, we also limit ours. Laws created to control do not stop controlling; they simply increase their sway to unrecognizable lengths. Some years ago, a small Indian tribe on an isolated Western reservation had its ancient treaty rights to hunt at will revoked. The reason for it was that the wild ducks they hunted traveled both interstate and internationally!

Controls are a poor substitute for responsibility. The whole point of our Christian faith is to foster the new man in Christ — a responsible man. George Washington preferred freedom to controls and therefore did not consider controls over a lying, libelous press. Our Biblical emphasis on responsibility has gone a long way towards making the United States a great nation.

Today, the world generally is choosing controls rather than freedom as the way to a good society. The world's solution to all problems is seen as another set of laws or controls. Instead of bettering things, the controls only worsen them.

The choice is before us: freedom or controls?

★ *three* ★

HAS THE FIRST AMENDMENT BEEN NULLIFIED?

HAS THE FIRST Amendment been rendered null and void by the Sixteenth—or Income Tax—Amendment?

Federal and state authorities are ready to argue that this is, in fact, the case. Listen to what the State of California Franchise Tax Board wrote to Pastor Harry Jackson of Calvary Baptist Church in Fairfield, California, on November 5, 1979:

> The Sixteenth Amendment authorizes Congress to levy a tax on income. There is no exclusion for churches so they have no constitutional exemption. There is a provision in the Internal Revenue Code, Section 501 (c) (3), for a statutory exemption.
>
> The state constitution is subservient to the federal constitution, so the above applies for state purposes. Article XIII, Sections 26 and 27, provide for the income and franchise tax, but it contains no provision for exemption for churches. Again, the exemption from state income tax is provided by state statute, not by the constitution. For state purposes, the statute is Section 23701d of the Revenue and Taxation Code.

As shown by the facts stated above, neither the federal nor state constitutions provide exemption from income tax for churches.

Consider what it means to say that churches have no constitutional exemption from income and other taxes, only a statutory one. The life of the church is then placed in the hands of the IRS and like agencies. Its freedom can be revoked at the will of a bureaucracy.

This is not an academic question. Pastor Harry Jackson's church, and about sixty others, had their tax exemptions revoked. For many of them, it began with their stand on a state proposition concerning homosexuality. This supposedly violated Form 199B, which forbids churches from taking a stand on ballot measures. Their tax exemptions were revoked, because they could not in good conscience sign the bureaucratic form. This meant these churches could then be sold for back taxes, which they refused to pay on constitutional grounds.

The only thing unusual about this case is that you did not read about it in the press. This should not surprise us. Many such cases go unpublicized. No civil government publicizes that it is taking away our liberties, nor does a subservient press herald such facts.

If the Sixteenth Amendment can be said to have wiped out the constitutional immunity of churches to taxation, it is easy enough to find in some other amendment or law reasons for curtailing freedom of speech, press, assembly, petition, and more. You can be sure that it is being done. In one area after another, our freedom is rapidly disappearing.

The Founding Fathers saw civil government as a dangerous power needing to be chained and restrained. We have been unchaining that power and feeding it with more and more taxes. Now we are in trouble.

The choice remains before us: freedom or controls?

★ *four* ★

IS THERE A NEW DEFINITION FOR DELINQUENCY?

I WAS A witness in a trial in a Midwestern state. On trial were the children of some families belonging to the Old Order of Mennonites. They were on trial for juvenile delinquency, although none of them had committed a single criminal offense. Their only crime was attendance at a Mennonite school. The school refused to submit to state controls which they rightly believed were humanistic and alien to their faith. As a result, the children were in court for the so-called crime of truancy.

The defense attorney asked for dismissal of the charges on the grounds that the state law did not define truancy as absence from a state controlled or approved school, but simply as truancy from school. Clearly, the children had not been truant from the Mennonite school. All the same, the motion for dismissal was denied, and the trial proceeded.

This was not an isolated case. Similar trials have taken place in other states. Some judges have stated that the child belongs to the state, not to the parents. Step by step, the state is claiming more and more powers over the family and its children.

The significant fact about all these trials is that it is children who rank among the very best in the community who are on trial. Moreover, the state puts more effort into trying to convict these children than it sometimes does with criminals and real delinquents.

The state seems to consider it a more serious offense to stay out of a state school than to endanger life and property. The state's power structure is affected every time a child leaves a state school for a Christian school, and this is the real offense.

Again and again, trials have shown that Christian schools provide at least as good an education, and in virtually every case, far better schooling than do the public schools. They produce better educated, more moral, and more resourceful graduates. In terms of comparison, the Christian schools clearly excel. Court-ordered testings have shown this.

However, there is a serious problem with Christian schools. They cut the amount of tax funds the state schools can demand, and state bureaucrats hate nothing more than any activity which limits their demand for taxes. For far less money, and at no cost to the taxpayer, the Christian school produces a better education. This is its offense. The state schools cannot stand the competition, so they strike back. As a result, Christian schools and churches are on trial all over the country, and their pupils are tried as delinquents.

Meanwhile, the state schools produce more and more illiterates. According to federal statistics, twenty-one million are functional illiterates. Estimates are that nine million more will graduate as illiterates before long. We have probably never had a higher illiteracy rate in this country.

Does it make good sense to prosecute the schools which do educate, or to take to juvenile courts children who are law-abiding and are guilty of nothing save attending a Christian school?

State and federal agencies are forcing controls upon us. Will you choose freedom?

★ *five* ★

JUSTICE IN THE COURTS?

IN MARCH OF 1980, a sheriff and his men arrested the pastor of a church in Mississippi. The Reverend Herman Fountain was pastor of the Bethel Baptist Church and Children's Home near Lucedale. The children's home sought to rehabilitate children or to provide a home for homeless children. No child was kept against his wishes, and the honor system prevailed.

A fifteen-year-old boy, six feet tall, about 180 pounds in weight, had just been placed in the home. Pastor Fountain had told the unruly boy either to keep the rules or leave. The boy took off, was picked up on the highway by the sheriff's men at 3 A.M. and 4 A.M., and claimed he had been "whipped." Without an investigation, the sheriff, some of his men, and a welfare department employee went to the church at 11 A.M. on Sunday morning to arrest the pastor. The assistant pastor was also arrested, the service shut down, and church records confiscated. All the children in the home were taken and stripped to see if they had any bruises.

No criminal action was proved or prosecuted. The state required minor changes of the home's facilities, most of them already planned or in progress, and asked Pastor and Mrs. Fountain (and three other defendants) to sign a "release" form stating that they would take no civil legal action charging violation of their civil and/or constitutional rights *before* they would agree to drop the charges.

What was unusual in this case was that the court apologized more than once, according to reports, to Pastor Fountain and the others.

Godly and innocent men are regularly subjected to legal injustice and harassment without any apologies. This Mississippi court was unusual in that some apology was made, and it deserves commendation for this fact.

What was usual in this case was what the "release" form represented. Our courts are agencies of county, state, or federal branches of government. They have come to represent and defend, not the freedom of the people or their interests, but those of the state and its bureaucracy.

As a result, the courts represent less and less a resort for the people in their appeal for justice, but more and more a statist resource against the people. A very high percentage of the cases heard by the higher courts represent appeals by some branch or agency of state against the people. We can be grateful, in this situation, that there are more than a few judges who vindicate the appeal, but the trend is towards the vindication of the state.

Marxism holds openly to the belief that the law and the courts must represent a class interest. Their charge against us is that our courts represent the capitalists against the workers. The theory behind our judicial system is that the court and law must represent justice, not a class or the state. The state cannot be identified with justice. All too often in history, past and present, the state has been the source of monstrous injustices.

For a court thus to protect any bureaucracy, agency, or officer and to cooperate in a release form which exempts all such from the rightful penalties for their actions, is wrong. The court has no right to represent the state or the people. It must represent justice.

★ *six* ★

DO WE HAVE TOO MANY LAWS?

PEOPLE ARE ALWAYS saying that "there ought to be a law" to take care of this or that matter. We are all surrounded by a number of problems, and we are all too ready to assume that a new law can solve the problem. We forget that we already have an abundance of laws.

Moreover, we forget what Charles Curtis once observed: "Language . . . in legal documents does not fix meaning. It circumscribes meaning. Legal interpretation is concerned, not with the meaning of words, but only with their boundaries." This means simply that any law passed means not what the lawmakers intended, but what lawyers, courts, and juries make it to mean. We pass a law to control criminals or child-abusers, and it very often ends up controlling us. The lawbreaker is very difficult and almost impossible to control. The law-abiding citizen is easy to control—he obeys the law. As a result, the bureaucracies created to enforce laws end up controlling those who are law-abiding!

This is why, on the whole, the only people controlled by the new laws we pass are us. The lawbreaker makes it his business to devise ways to get around the law. The tax-evader makes evasion an art, and often a legal one. Those of us who have no protection against a bureaucracy or a court wind up as the losers.

The more laws we pass, the more we are taxed and the more we are controlled. People constantly rail at bureaucrats—even lawmakers do. What all forget is that almost all laws require either the expansion or creation of a bureaucracy to define and enforce the law. To ask for another law is to ask for more bureaucracy and more taxes. When we say,

"There ought to be a law," we are also saying that there ought to be more bureaucracy and more taxes.

The bureaucracy then helps define the law by the way it applies it, interprets it, and enforces it. By and large, most of the laws governing us are bureaucratic regulations. Congress, the state, and local lawmaking bodies annually pass a limited number of laws. For each page of laws, bureaucracies put out thousands of pages of interpretation and regulation.

As a result, we now have more laws and regulations governing us than any man can know, or possibly understand, including lawyers. Some years ago, lawyers had to specialize in a particular branch of law: corporate law, tax law, trust law, criminal law, and so on. Now lawyers are specializing in specialized areas of specialties!

Very definitely, you will not improve matters by asking for another law!

Why this mess? Is it not because men have come to expect too much from law? It is faith and character which make men free, not laws. Normally, we do not eliminate problems by legislation, but rather by our godly lives and actions. Laws cannot save us. It is undue trust in law which is creating problems for us. Men create laws as though law could be their savior.

★ *seven* ★

WHAT IS A WITNESS?

OUR SYSTEM OF legal justice is increasingly in trouble in both the criminal courts and the civil courts. There are many reasons for this problem, but for the present let us concentrate on one, the witness.

In any case, the witness is perhaps the most important single factor. Attorneys bring to a case their legal knowledge and a planned and researched defense. The lawyer knows only as much of a case as he is told. The judge also brings to a case his knowledge of the law, as well as the responsibility to define the law as it relates to the case, keep the conduct of the case within the law, and, unless there is a jury, to render a decision.

However, no decision can be made without evidence. All the evidence is provided by witnesses. This makes the witness the key factor in the legal process. This should tell us why there is a problem in our courts today. Witnesses do not take their responsibility seriously enough. They often appear reluctantly and with little appreciation of their importance. I have often seen witnesses who had a great deal of knowledge about the case content themselves with inadequate answers: a yes or no, a short sentence which says all too little, and a general feeling of wanting to get off the stand as quickly as possible.

A witness provides the evidence which makes a decision possible. Without the witnesses, neither side has a case. We have no right to complain about the results of a trial if we do not do our duty faithfully when we are witnesses.

But this is not all. A good witness can help change the law. When a law is passed, its meaning is then established by court-room decisions which stand or are made in higher courts. It is the evidence presented which throws light on the question on trial and provides the material for case law. Case law — the decisions which determine, develop, or limit a statute — depends heavily on the testimony provided by witnesses.

One case in which I appeared as a witness in 1978 was appealed to that state's supreme court, and then, in 1986, to the U.S. Supreme Court. The testimonies of those of us who appeared as witnesses may have proved to be decisive in one of the most important cases in the country today.

Because of our system of case laws, the witness has an important part to play in the lawmaking process. We have no right to complain about bad laws or bad decisions if we refuse to play our part as witnesses when called to do so.

The very word *witness* has an important history and meaning. It is basic to the New Testament and to the life of the early church. We still speak commonly of witnessing to our faith.

A true witness speaks for the truth. The purpose of an honest witness is to bring that aspect of the truth which he knows to the attention of the law. Good witnesses thus provide for a meeting and union between law and truth. We cannot afford unwilling witnesses: they are a disaster for both truth and the law.

★ *eight* ★

DONE ANY JURY DUTY LATELY?

ONE OF THE first reactions of many people to a jury-duty summons is to try to get excused. After all, jury duty does not pay much, it takes time away from our work and activities, and most cases are definitely on the dull side.

All too often, the same person who complains about jury duty also complains about our rotten courts, bad decisions, and what's wrong with our country. They forget that our form of civil government places much of the decision-making power into the hands of the people. Jury duty gives the people a tremendous power. It is significant that we call it a duty and not a privilege. Not many people summoned for jury duty would appear if the summons lacked a legal clout — but it is a privilege.

In a jury trial, the jury is the final judge. This is a tremendous power, and a very basic one to our form of government. The function of a judge in a jury trial is to explain the law to the jury and to indicate the jury's areas of jurisdiction.

Even more, very few agencies in the American form of civil government have powers approaching those of a grand jury.

However, when I looked up the subject of juries in a 400-page book on law for laymen, I found there was indeed a section on jury duty, but its title was, "Exemption from Jury Duty." Apparently all that most readers want to know about jury duty is how to get out of it. A handbook on law for ministers gives a brief sketch of the kinds of juries, and not much more. School books, including textbooks on the Constitution, are not too much better.

The important fact is that the jury system was one of our greatest means of establishing the people's freedom from statist and legal injustices and tyrannies. We talk much today about freedom of speech and freedom of press, and rightly so. They are important. However, the Bill of Rights, in the First Amendment, gives us six words on freedom of speech, and only four on freedom of the press. On the other hand, not only is the jury mentioned in the Fifth Amendment, but it is the subject of the Sixth and Seventh Amendments.

Very plainly, the American people in 1791 regarded the jury as central and basic to their freedom. They would have found our unconcern horrifying and dangerous. Both then and later, there were many who held that the greater freedom enjoyed by the peoples of England and America was largely a product of the jury system. They would have insisted that a sound jury system and responsible jurors are necessary for a people to be free from a repressive and unjust civil government.

Juries in those days were seen as a defense against judges, as well as against bureaucrats and rulers. The people then held that a judge, as an officer of civil government, could become an agent of the state rather than of justice. We have problems now not only with rulers and bureaucrats, but with judges *and* juries. After all, a jury is a powerful instrument only in the hands of a *free* people. However, if a people do not want to be free, the jury system grows weaker and weaker, as it has today.

★ *nine* ★

WHAT KIND OF PROTECTION DO WE NEED?

THE FOUNDING FATHERS of this country, led by George Washington, recognized that we the people need protection. Part of our problem today is that we have changed our idea of protection.

The Constitutional Convention and its members believed that a federal government should be strong enough to provide unity and a defense from foreign and domestic enemies. On the other hand, they were afraid of a federal government which could be so powerful that it would threaten the freedom of the states and the people.

As a result, they wrote a constitution with the intention, *first* of all, of chaining and limiting the powers of the federal government. They truly believed that people need protection, not only from hoodlums and foreign enemies, but from their own civil government. In fact, the people felt so strongly about this need for protection from the federal government that they insisted on spelling it out more fully than the Constitution did. As a result, the Bill of Rights was immediately added to provide that protection from the federal power.

Clearly, they held that freedom provides a better protection than a power-hungry federal government, and they moved to safeguard freedom.

Second, they believed in granting only limited powers to the state to protect the people from crime and disorders. However, they definitely did not believe that any civil government can prevent (in any effective way) the rise of social disorder. Washington and most other founders believed that no legislation could replace the need for good character. As a result, those men spoke of the basic need for Christian faith and sound moral character as the basic safeguard for any country.

A lawless people will not be restrained by laws. A godly people do not need a policeman on every corner to keep them in line. In the 1930s, one town of less than 5,000 people had one policeman, a relief man, and virtually no crime. An arrest was a rarity. Today, with only 900 more people, there are eighteen police in patrol cars, an office staff, and problems. The difference is in the people. The town now has more laws and controls, but it is definitely not as good as it was then. The difference between then and now lies in the families, the churches, and the schools. Doubling the police force again will not help much, because the deterioration in the faith and the character of the people continues.

Now they have a problem, not only with crime, but with too much civil government. The families in that community want protection, but how can you protect people from themselves?

In other words, we are looking for the wrong kind of protection. The protection we need cannot be provided by the state; attempts to get it by law only rob us of our freedom.

The protection we need comes from a godly faith and character, not from Washington, D.C., or the state capitol. Nothing is more necessary for the flourishing of the protection we need than *freedom* — it is the seedbed of faith and character.

★ *ten* ★

WHAT'S WRONG WITH OUR POLITICIANS?

IT IS AN election year again, and we are once more deluged with campaign promises and electioneering. It has also become more popular than ever to abuse the politicians, ridicule them, and poke fun at them.

To a certain degree, this is understandable. All too many politicians talk as though their election would save the world and usher in the millennium. Their speeches tend to be full of promises as to what they will do for us. However, we need to ask ourselves this question: why do they do it? Is it not because the people are demanding more and more, and electing those candidates who promise the most?

One state senator sent out a questionnaire to all the voters in his district to give them an opportunity to tell him what they wanted. The results he got were like many others all over the country. The people wanted lower taxes and more benefits! Their pressures on the senator made it clear that usually they preferred more benefits. Perhaps it would be more accurate to say that they preferred more benefits for themselves and their area, and less for all others, so they could have lower taxes and benefits both!

The sad fact is that the politicians give the people what they want, and the people still complain. I am reminded of a man who demanded steaks or roasts daily, and then nagged his wife because she always needed more money. He insisted on paying less and demanding more!

The politicians will give us what we really want, but we are not willing enough to admit that we the people have voted ourselves into trouble. We do need better politicians, but we also need better voters.

One of Oliver Cromwell's chaplains, Puritan preacher Hugh Peter, saw the problem clearly in his day and summed it up in these words: "Good men, not good laws, must save kingdoms." An old proverb also states it with clarity and bluntness in declaring: "One cannot fill a torn sack." If our national life and character is like a torn sack, we are in trouble.

What an election does is to bring us face to face with all our national problems, sins, and errors. If we feel that the politicians on the ballot are a bad lot, then we need to ask ourselves why they were voted in. Why do we as a people have a knack for getting ourselves into more and more trouble?

Some years ago, I knew briefly a woman who had been married and divorced six times. She claimed that all six of the men were bad characters, really terrible people to live with, and guilty of all kinds of unfaithfulness and abuse. From friends and a local pastor, I learned that what she had said about all six of the men was true. The woman claimed that she had had nothing but "bad luck" with men! But six bad marriages is not bad luck—it is a perfect record of bad judgment, bad taste, and bad character. There was no hope for that woman, because the one conclusion she would not make was that there was something wrong with her faith, moral judgment, and standards.

The same applies to us. If we vote in bad politicians again and again, something is wrong with us also.

★ *eleven* ★

WHAT MAKES A QUACK?

SOME TIME AGO, I saw some old-time medicine show ads. The medicines advertised each claimed remarkable healing powers. One in particular had a long list of ailments which it declared it could heal, including tuberculosis, female complaints, rheumatism, impotence, and about ten things more. This and other like ads were fun to read. What made people believe in such quackery?

Before we say that people were more gullible in those days, let us consider what quackery is. Perhaps we are even more gullible than people were a century ago. There is some reason to believe that ours is the great age of quackery.

The difference between a quack doctor and a good one begins with a sense of limitation. A quack medicine and a quack doctor promise too much. This is why some of our wonder drugs, including perhaps the pill, border at times on quackery — they promise too much. A sound medicine offers limited help for a limited and specific problem. It works no miracles. It cannot replace good hygiene and sound nutrition. Similarly, the doctor who promises the least is the wiser doctor, because he recognizes how limited his role is.

The more we demand of a medicine or a doctor, the more likely we are to fall prey to quackery. It is sound medical practice which offers the more modest and specific goals.

Today, we demand quacks in one area of life after another because we make exorbitant and unreasonable demands.

One such area is politics. If we expect the politician to be a combination of a savior, a perfect ruler, a promoter of prosperity and of perfect law and order, we are asking for a quack. What a state legislator or congressman can do is actually very limited (and the more limited the better). Once elected, he is assigned to some committees, to become a specialist in very limited areas such as some aspect of agriculture, foreign trade, law enforcement, or the like. At his best, he can work to clear obstructions and free some area of activity from the controls of the omnipotent state. If he becomes a quack, he will pass laws to try to cure every imaginable problem: laws to end poverty, unemployment, social conflicts, and the like. He will try to create agencies to take care of all the problems of education, health, labor and management conflicts, welfare, and the like. The more the law promises to give us, the more popular it is. What we laugh at in the old patent medicines, we demand from our politicians.

The old medicine show is with us still. It has simply changed locations. Its new locale is the political circuit, where, by popular demand, the new medicine men promise all kinds of cures, if we will only give our votes and money.

What makes a quack? Why, we do, every time and everywhere, when we demand more of medicine, or of politics, or of anything else than can sensibly be expected. We have quackery in politics because we demand it. We have created a market for it.

★ *twelve* ★

THE WAR AGAINST FREEDOM

RECENTLY, A CASE went to court in which a federal agency sought to compel a theological seminary to conform to the Equal Employment Opportunity Commission (EEOC) hiring or employment requirements. The seminary in question was the Southern Baptist Theological Seminary. All employees of the seminary must be Southern Baptist members or of similar denominations, and all faculty appointments are made in terms of godliness as well as scholastic merit. To this, the EEOC objected.

The court ruled that the EEOC did not have jurisdiction over the seminary, because the curriculum and the school are clearly religious. Because the school had submitted to accreditation for Veteran's Administration benefits, and to the Texas Department of Education's spot checks, the EEOC held that the school had waived its First Amendment protection.

Although this case resulted in a victory for the seminary, the victory is limited to that case. There is no reason to believe that various state and federal agencies will not continue their efforts to control Christian colleges and seminaries. Everything points to an increase on all fronts of efforts to control the church and all kinds of religious institutions. We are facing an increasing war against all freedom of religion.

I myself, as a witness in a number of cases, have heard the state attorneys refer to the First Amendment as a document of historical interest only. One such attorney insisted that a "dynamic" view of constitutional law and development requires us to see the necessity for federal and state controls. In his thinking, all meaning in the First Amendment as we have known it is null and void. In other words, freedom of religion, press, speech, assembly, and petition should be subject to careful and strict controls. There are even some who hold that it should be illegal for the people to try to influence their congressman or senators. For all such people, the great enemy is freedom.

Now, it is very true that freedom can be and is commonly abused. It is easy to chronicle the abuses of freedom. However, the abuses of power and of controls are far more common, and far greater. We cannot have perfection this side of heaven; it is a mistake to hope for it. The demand for power to control is based on the belief that abuses can be eliminated, given enough regulation. This is a deadly belief.

The only people who are never out of line are in a graveyard. Every attempt to regulate and control men into a perfect society gives us instead a graveyard society. In the name of a new heaven, such regulators put us in hell instead.

There is a war going on against freedom. The basic freedom is religious liberty. If we lose that, we are then a slave people, living in a slave state. Now, more than ever, we need to help those fighting in defense of the First Amendment.

★ SERIES TWO ★

★ *one* ★

IS THE FIRST AMENDMENT BEING MISREPRESENTED?

A NUMBER OF groups have attacked the church and churchmen for getting involved in politics. These criticisms are particularly aimed against evangelical groups formed to deal with various moral issues and legal attacks on churches and Christian schools. These critics charge that such activities are a violation of the First Amendment and the separation of church and state.

However, the First Amendment was written to prevent the establishment of a national church by the federal government. A substantial number of Americans in 1781 were foreign-born or had close ties with either Britain or continental Europe. They knew that a state church easily and readily becomes a corrupt church because it is not answerable to the people. Even more, they knew that when a civil government establishes and supports a church financially, that church will tend to be silent where civil corruption is concerned. When financially supported by the state, it will usually be unwilling to criticize or indict the hand that feeds it.

The American War for Independence was extensively condoned by the colonial clergy. They were opposed to the establishment by Parliament or the British Crown of a state church. The colonial clergy were vocal in calling attention to the moral failures of British royal rule.

As a result, the colonists felt very strongly, when the Constitution was adopted, that the great need of the United States was a free church in a free state. They wanted a free church precisely because they felt the need for a strong and independent voice to call attention to the religious and moral issues in politics. They felt it was necessary for the church to speak freely and effectively without being silenced by state control. The whole purpose of the First Amendment was thus to make sure that the church would have a free and uncontrolled voice in public affairs.

The colonists were afraid of "big government." They were even more afraid of the combination of a powerful civil government and a state church. The independence of the church was to help ensure the protection of the people from a power-hungry state. In fact, both in colonial and early constitutional America, an important aspect of church life was the preaching of election sermons, to spell out the moral and religious issues at stake in civil and political affairs. It would be a disaster if that moral voice were silenced.

★ *two* ★

CAN THE STATE PRESCRIBE A PLAN OF SALVATION?

IN ONE OF the trials in which I appeared as a witness, a church which operated a children's home for delinquents was in court because the state demanded that a humanistic plan of salvation be taught to all the children. This home had a remarkable record for rehabilitation: over 90 percent of the children who passed through its doors for about thirty years are both law-abiding and Christian. Many are now active in the ministry. The state-operated homes have a record of failure in over 90 percent of cases. The failures — the state-operated welfare agencies — are seeking to control the successes — the Christian homes.

The state took the pastor and his homes to court because, instead of psychotherapy, the Bible and Jesus Christ are used to save the children. In other words, the state and its welfare agencies sought to prescribe the plan of salvation which these Christian homes for delinquents must use. Their prescribed plan is plainly humanistic.

There are two important issues at stake here. *First,* the First Amendment is being set aside, in that we clearly have an establishment of religion. Welfare agencies across the country operate on a humanistic religious premise and with a humanistic plan of salvation. Tax funds are thus used to promote a religion most Americans do not confess or affirm — humanism.

Second, this state-supported and financed religion is persecuting Christianity and trying to force its welfare agencies out of existence.

Its premise is that only the humanistic plan of salvation has the right to exist.

This premise is not openly stated. It is disguised in the name of various regulations. We are treated to a barrage of propaganda about the supposed abuses which are found in these Christian homes, charges which fail to stand up under investigation.

The plain fact is that we have two rival plans of salvation at war today. Humanism seeks to discredit and destroy Christianity and capture America for itself. We have thus a religious war under way in the United States: humanism versus Christianity. Your future will be determined by the outcome of that battle.

★ *three* ★

DOES AMERICA HAVE AN ESTABLISHED RELIGION?

IT IS INCREASINGLY apparent that the United States has an established religion which uses tax funds to promote itself and so gain converts. This religion is humanism.

Humanism has full possession of the public (or state) schools of the United States, and these tax-supported institutions are teaching the religion of humanism to the children in their charge. In some states, state boards of education have even attempted to compel Christian schools to use state textbooks which teach humanism. Whether he likes it or not, the American taxpayer is paying for the support and propagation of humanism when he is taxed for education.

All the state and federal welfare agencies are also operated on humanistic premises and are dominated by humanists. Their enormous tax-funded budgets promote plans for the rehabilitation or salvation of people in terms of a humanistic plan of salvation. Few things in history have been more dismal failures than our welfarism, but this does not discourage fanatical humanists. They keep demanding more money to make even more damaging failures.

All of this, however, is very damaging to you also. The greater part of your tax dollar goes for education and welfare. This means that, whether you like it or not, you are paying out several tithes each year to finance a humanistic plan of salvation.

The cost to you is financially great, but it is even greater in terms of the moral damage done to you and to our country by humanism. Ideas do have consequences. False doctrines lead to false conclusions and to a false and destructive way of life. Today, besides dominating our state schools and our welfare programs, humanism dominates our foreign policy, our bureaucracies, many of our courts, the IRS, and more. Humanism finances its plan of salvation at the taxpayer's expense, and it resents the slightest attempt by Christians to alter the present course of affairs.

We do have an established religion, and its name is humanism. Is this what you want? You *are* paying for it, like it or not, and you will continue to do so until you decide to change things.

★ *four* ★

ARE PSYCHOLOGY AND PSYCHIATRY SCIENTIFIC?

ARE PSYCHOLOGY AND psychiatry deserving of the classification of science? Is psychotherapy valid, or a genuine method of healing and understanding?

Obviously, some people have a great deal of faith in psychologists and counselors trained in psychotherapy. Some doctors recommend psychotherapy for mentally troubled patients. The Veteran's Administration, and other civil agencies, rely on it. Court-ordered examinations of criminal offenders are an important part of many trials. Many seminaries and churches train their pastors in psychotherapeutic methodologies.

Increasingly, however, men within psychology and psychiatry are challenging the basic premises of their disciplines. One key figure has been the psychiatrist, Dr. Thomas Szasz, M.D., who has attacked the very idea of mental sickness. More recently psychologists Dr. Martin Bobgan, and Deidre Bobgan, have added their weight to this challenge. The problem, as they and others point out, is not mental sickness, but sin.

The Hans J. Eysenck study showed that psychotherapy is not effective in treating mental disorders. In fact, people are more likely to improve if they avoid all forms of psychotherapy. The evidence indicates that psychotherapy can be harmful. The Bobgans conclude that psychotherapy is not a science. Jay Ziskin, a Californian State University psychologist, in discussing psychiatric examinations of criminals, has said a diagnosis trying to determine the mental condition of a criminal at the time of the crime is more likely to be wrong than not.

The Bobgans, in their book, *The Psychological Way/The Spiritual Way*, remind us that the Biblical way of dealing with mental and moral problems is and has always been the most effective. It is the one enduring method of coping with man's problems. Except where physical diseases create problems calling for medical relief, man's problems have as their cause a religious problem. To seek relief from a moral problem in nonmoral means is to aggravate the problem.

But psychotherapy is powerful because it is humanism in action, and our humanistic urge wants to deal with our problems by means of humanism. Psychotherapy is thus an alien plan of salvation and an enemy to Christianity.

★ *five* ★

WERE THERE CHRISTIANS IN THE CONTINENTAL ARMIES?

IN 1832, ABOUT fifty years after the War for Independence ended, Congress passed a pension act for the veterans of that war. The applicants were interviewed, and their stories were recorded by a court reporter or clerk. Some of these recorded stories, edited by John. C. Dann, have been published recently under the title *The Revolution Remembered: Eyewitness Accounts of the War for Independence.*

Something is at once apparent upon reading these accounts: almost none of the applicants for pensions were churchgoers. Does this mean that Christians were absent from the ranks of soldiers during the War for Independence? Were there no Christians with Washington at Valley Forge or elsewhere? Were not most Americans supposed to be Christians in those days? How do we account for the absence of Christians in these narratives?

The answer is a surprisingly simple one. Almost all the Christian veterans refused to apply for pensions. Many churches then were against any Christian receiving public funds. They took very seriously the requirement of 1 Timothy 5:8 "[I]f any provide not for his own, and specially those of this own house, he hath denied the faith, and is worse than an infidel." These churches believed it was necessary for a family to care for its own needy members, and, lacking godly relatives, a man's fellow believers must care for him. As a result, there were few churchgoers among these first American pensioners. The church then stood for something.

Today, although 53.8 percent of all adults eighteen years old and above profess to be born again Christians, not half of them can name five of the Ten Commandments. (How many can you name, by the way?) They stand for next to nothing because they know next to nothing about faith. They "have" it as a form of life insurance.

We also have—in 1980—numerous politicians who profess to be born-again Christians. It seems to make very little, if any, difference to their lives and politics. Like all too many Americans, they are warm bodies in church, not living souls.

But without the faith, the character necessary for freedom quickly disappears. No politician can make much difference to a country. It take a free people to create the climate of freedom, and today we have a people who regard it as smart to get all they can out of the public trough. As a result, freedom is giving way to slavery. How many churches today who claim to be faithful would stand in terms of 1 Timothy 5:8 as the churches of 1832 did?

★ *six* ★

DID THE ROMANS, AND DO THE AMERICANS, LOVE VIRTUE?

THE EARLY ROMAN love of virtue gave way, in time, to a love of evil. Not many Romans, however, liked to admit that this had happened. Instead of an open love for evil, they disguised their taste for sin with a supposed desire to expose wrongdoings. As a result, exposés of evil in high places became very popular. Writers, both important and unimportant, found that the sins of the high and mighty made for a large readership. Most Romans loved to profess outrage over the sins of the mighty, when in fact they envied them. Writers like Tacitus, Suetonius, and others had a ready market for their accounts of sin in high places.

Senate investigations also became popular. Every time there was a hearing on evil in public office, many people assumed that a great forward step had been taken. The false assumption was very widespread that condemning evil made a man righteous.

This is a dangerous belief. No man becomes righteous or moral by condemning sin in other people. The Bible tells us in Psalm 11:7: "[T]he righteous LORD loveth righteousness." We are not told that God blesses men for their interest in evil, but only when they are righteous (Deut. 28).

Today, this failing of the Romans is our failing also. We have come to believe that our denunciation of evil means righteousness on our part, and we have men on the left and right of political issues who think they are good because they are loud in denouncing evil. More than a few periodicals have been very successful, like many politicians, simply for exposing and denouncing evil. Well, Rome always had a loud chorus of denouncers and perished all the same. Then as now, the ability to investigate, denounce, and condemn evil is no guarantee of righteousness.

The Romans of old, like Americans of today, loved to see evil exposed. They loved to talk about national scandals. Evil is interesting to most people, whereas righteousness is not. At a dinner party, a suddenly disgusted host said, "Let's stop all this talk about scandals and evils. Let's talk about something good for a change!" The result was a painful silence. No one was interested in talking about righteousness. But freedom rests on righteousness (or justice). Without righteousness, freedom perishes.

★ *seven* ★

DO WE WANT TO BE LIED TO?

THE VIETNAM WAR has been over for some years, and American troops have returned home to be forgotten, but one story from that war still remains in my mind. A young Marine, loaded with morphine, was carried into the Danang Marine Hospital. Both his legs were gone, but he did not know it. He became conscious briefly, and saw a chaplain standing over him. He asked the chaplain, "Are my legs okay?" "Sure," said the chaplain, although he knew better. By the next day, the young Marine knew better, and when the chaplain came by, he called him the dirtiest name he could think of. It is a hard story to forget.

I thought of it again when I heard someone who manages political campaigns say that the people want to be lied to, and too much truth-telling is a good way to lose elections. Very few people, he said, really want to know how bad things are.

Is this true? Do we want to be lied to? Well, all too often I am told, "Don't tell Mom that Dad is dying," or, "Don't tell my parents that my brother is dying," and so on.

A friend of mine, knowing economics, predicted to his relatives what would happen to our economy and to their investments. They refused to listen to him. When he turned out to be right, they turned on him, saying, "It's people who talk like you who make bad things happen!"

I know several ministers who lost churches for dealing very Biblically and patiently with the sins of the congregation. One vicious reprobate stood up in a congregational meeting and called to dismiss the pastor, declaring, "His preaching doesn't make me feel good." Given the flagrant sins of that man, no true preaching would ever make him feel good!

All too many people want lies that make them feel good. The prophet Isaiah spoke of an evil generation which demanded of God's prophets, "[S]peak unto us smooth things, prophesy deceit" (Isa. 30:10). But lies are the death of truth and freedom. People who want to be lied to are candidates for defeat and slavery.

Do you want to be lied to, or do you want the truth? Do you shut the door on unpleasant facts and try to put a good front on things? The Pharisees of old tried to whitewash evil, but it did not work then, nor will it work now.

Faith and freedom require of us a love for the truth and a rejection of lies.

There is no comfort in a lie, only bitterness. The chaplain who lied to the Marine did not restore his legs with his lie; he did destroy the trust between them, and all future relationship.

★ *eight* ★

DO WE WANT A MONOPOLY IN EDUCATION?

A STEP WAS proposed by the Ontario government in Canada, which some believe the United States will also take before too long. The Ontario legislature considered a bill which would make it illegal for anyone but a state-operated university to grant degrees (*Presbyterian Journal,* July 30, 1980, 6). Similar efforts have been made in the United States with respect to children's homes, nurseries, grade schools, and high schools. Basic to these efforts is the belief that only the state is competent to pass judgment on or to produce quality educational instructions.

The sad fact is that state institutions are far from the best and are often the worst. State accreditation is no evidence of quality—often it means the reverse. Some of our most famous private universities, like Harvard, have never been accredited! Why should they submit to their inferiors?

The idea that the state has some special wisdom which enables it to pass judgment on everything is a dangerous doctrine. The state is not God, nor does it have any special competence or wisdom.

If the Ontario measure passes, every Christian college in Ontario, and every private college, will become illegal. Education, like the postal service, will become a state monopoly.

Few things are more arrogant and inefficient than a true monopoly. It has an enforced power and a guaranteed market. Quality becomes less and less a consideration. All over the world, however, civil governments are working to gain a monopoly control over education, economics, planning, and more. Another word for this is totalitarianism.

To gain this control, statists warn of abuses in the private sector. These abuses are sometimes real and sometimes invented. We regularly read about bureaucratic charges against some private agency, but we too seldom read when these charges are proven false. Such stories are back-page news at best.

Meanwhile, the closer the state comes to gaining a monopoly over any area, the more corrupt its performance becomes, and the more incompetent. The goal of statist controls is not better service but greater power.

Education was once entirely controlled by the non-statist sector. The state was a complete outsider to the school. By its entrance into education, the state gained a power of mind control over the younger generation, and this power is increasingly used to foster statism, not freedom. We have gained by the separation of church and state. Why shouldn't we again have a separation of school and state? It *is* necessary for the preservation of freedom.

★ *nine* ★

DO WE BELIEVE IN INCOMPETENCE?

A MAN IS known by his actions, or, as our Lord states it in the Sermon on the Mount, "by their fruits ye shall know them" (Matt. 7:20). If a person makes the same mistake over and over again, it tells us something about that person. As I previously mentioned, I once met a woman who had been married and divorced six times; every one of her husbands turned out to be a beast or brute, she claimed. I learned later that she was telling the truth. However, she also claimed that she was "unlucky in love." That was definitely not the truth; she was *not* "unlucky in love"; she was just plain stupid.

Are we as a nation somewhat like that woman? She had a taste for bad men; we seem to have a national taste for bad politicians.

Even worse, we have a faith in politics, and we believe that politics and civil government can give us the good life. This is about as intelligent an opinion as believing that hell is an air-conditioned resort.

Throughout the long centuries of human history, when civil government has not been tyrannical, oppressive, and confiscatory, it has been at best just plain incompetent. Of course, only when civil governments have been too weak to be oppressive have they been relatively and mildly good. The history of civil governments is the long history of tyranny.

In fact, more than a few people have said that the one real ability any civil government has ever possessed has been to take money from people and to waste it. State and federal agencies are very successful in taxing us and not much else. Why, then, ask for more from civil government? Do we believe in giving more power to incompetents? Have we money to burn, that we are ready to increase the powers of the state and federal governments?

That woman with six bad ex-husbands was looking for lucky number seven; she was a cashier in a gambling casino. Are we any smarter if we go on giving greater powers to Washington, D.C., and the state capitol, while expecting something good to come to us? We lose both our money and our freedom, and the federal and state governments gain in power and in money.

Obviously, we must believe in the virtues of incompetence, tyranny, waste, and mismanagement because we continue to look to civil misgovernment to save and bless us.

★ *ten* ★

IS THE FIRST AMENDMENT BEING USED TO PERSECUTE CHRISTIANS?

ON HUNDREDS OF state college and university campuses across the country, a major threat faces campus religious ministries which are Christian. In two federal district courts, judges have ruled that state universities may not allow such religious use of their facilities. In one case, the Christian student group was told that it could use campus facilities for a nonreligious party, or if for religious use, only twice in a quarter, with application and payment of rent. One person remarked, "It's almost as if we pay rent if we use the word 'God'; but if we add the word 'damn,' it's free." In other cases, public high schools have sought to bar Christian student groups from meeting on the premises during lunch, after school, or at any time.

In other words, if your religion is atheism or humanism, you may use school or university facilities, but not if you are a Christian.

All this is done in the name of the First Amendment and the separation of church and state. But this is not all. When Christians in California organized as Californians for Biblical Morality, one newspaper called this a violation of the First Amendment. In other words, it is all right for homosexuals or prostitutes to organize for legal action, but Christians should be forbidden to attempt to influence politics.

The plain implication is that any one may have all the freedom he wants, and use public infrastructure also, *provided* he is not a Christian. In the name of the First Amendment, freedom is denied to Christians.

Why should campus Marxists, atheists, humanists, and homosexuals have freedom, but not Christian students? What kind of judges are we appointing to the bench, that they use the First Amendment to deny freedom to Christians?

Years ago, someone said fascism would come to the United States in the name of fighting fascism to save freedom. I was reminded of that when I learned that someone who wants freedom denied to Christian groups insisted that he is thereby fighting fascism!

The days of freedom are numbered in the United States if such things continue. And continue they will as long as most people are indifferent to the growth of bigger and bigger civil government and the decline of our freedom. Are we any better off today for having concentrated so much statist power in Washington, D.C., and the state capitol? Unless we begin to change things, we will soon be no more than slaves of the state.

★ *eleven* ★

ARE WE ENCOURAGING INSANITY?

WE ARE HEARING increasingly all kinds of opinions which bear the marks of insanity. Thus one feminist leader has said that we must work for uterus implants in men, to enable men to bear children, and so achieve sexual equality (Phyllis Chesler). A professor of anthropology has charged that the old expression of abandoning ship, "women and children first," represents male manipulative psychology whose purpose is the exploitation of women (*Montagu in Amneus*). Another man, looking at women's liberation, has said that the answer is to keep women barefoot and pregnant, and when he continued, it was obvious that his serious thoughts were worse.

Why is such wild and insane thinking so commonplace? There is scarcely an issue on the national scene without wild and absurd remarks coming from all quarters. Sometimes it is embarrassing to listen to or read widely held opinions on the current scene. They sound insane. What is behind all this?

I recall hearing, some years ago, many like wild statements, but they came from children—spoiled, bratty children, at that. They were threats: "If you don't do this, I'm going to run away," or some such thing. Now, it's "do what we say, or we'll demonstrate and riot." With children, these are wild and impossible statements made without any sense of responsibility or reality. Now we hear this from adults.

Childishness and foolishness from a child are bad enough, but in an adult it is insanity. For a parent to give in to a child is bad enough. For a society or a country to give in to the tantrums of adults is deadly. It is a way of saying that we will not be ruled by the slow, sometimes irritating processes of social order, but by threats and tantrums. To be ruled by such is to destroy freedom.

God knows I do not like much of what goes on in this country. The courts often scare me with their indifference to justice and their overattention to technicalities. The answer to this is not tantrums or violence. If our society is not any better than it is, it is quite likely because we, as a people, are no better than we have to be, and far from mature. Can we expect just courts in the midst of an unjust, lawless, and immature people?

Any time something is radically wrong with a society, you can be sure that something is also wrong with the people. To change things, begin with yourself, and that does not mean throwing a tantrum. To encourage social insanities is to destroy freedom.

★ *twelve* ★

ARE WE WATERING DOWN OUR MONEY?

WE ARE TOLD that, in bygone years, milk was mixed with water before it was sold. This was clearly a dishonest practice, and we can be grateful that it is ended. We have today, thanks to the federal government, a far more deadly practice: watered down or diluted money. The result of this is *inflation*.

Inflation is an increase in the money supply by means of printing-press money and excess of credit. Inflation is the watering down of money to cheat the public. Everyone who has a savings account, a pension or retirement plan, a life insurance policy, or any monetary assets, is robbed. Each year, his assets are worth less.

Inflation is a form of larceny. It eventually robs people of all their monetary assets. For a time, it rewards the debtors, because it enables people to pay off good debts with bad money as money gets cheaper. Inflation, however, finally wipes out everyone through the inability of income to keep pace with double-digit inflation, confiscatory taxation, economic disruptions, and the like.

The worst destruction wrought by inflation is of *freedom*. Because the federal government is the source of inflation — of money creation — it controls more and more of the nation's wealth and, by taxation, more and more of its income. The federal government increases its power and decreases our freedom. By creating fiat money, the federal government plays the role of a legalized counterfeiter.

Accelerating inflation is the prelude to a number of evils: totalitarianism, economic controls, social unrest and moral decay, revolutionary activities, and more. Inflation has its roots in bad morality—it is a belief that larceny can be good if controlled by the government. Inflation is born out of bad morals, and it creates even worse morals. It corrupts society.

Moreover, freedom dies as a result. The purpose of the U.S. Constitution, according to the Founding Fathers, was to chain the federal government in order to keep the people free. Now the federal government is chaining the people and seeking freedom from all restraints on its power. If we do not halt inflation, we will lose more than money. We will lose our freedom.

★ SERIES THREE ★

★ *one* ★

DO WE TRUST IN BUREAUCRATS?

THE *Wall Street Journal* ("Review of the News," September 17, 1980, 61) recently reported on a case of theft. A man stole a snow plow from his employer, and he confessed to the crime when the police came by. Because the police failed to tell him of his right to silence before his confession, the thief went free. In the second act of this story, the employer fired the confessed thief, but an arbitrator ordered the worker reinstated.

Another incident: I was a witness in a federal courtroom in a case involving Christian schools and the federal government's demand that all such schools become a part of the federal unemployment insurance program. Under cross-examination, two Labor Department officials admitted that it was their intention to review and control all firing policies. Thus, if a teacher were fired by a Christian school for molesting a child (or another reason, such as denying the faith), they reserved the right to order his reinstatement.

Behind all this is the hidden premise that civil government is wiser and more moral than the rest of us, and hence better able to give justice in all such matters. Is this true?

Some years ago, I went to school with some who later became state and federal bureaucrats. Most of them were rather inferior men. What gave them special powers to judge more wisely than the rest of us once they took their civil service jobs? Did something happen to give these men sudden wisdom? They were no better (and often worse) than the rest of us in running their own lives. Do civil servants undergo some kind of federal pentecost whereby wisdom descends upon them from on high? What makes them think they can run our lives better than we can?

This is, of course, the premise of statism: Big Brother can do it better for you than you can, therefore, all power to Big Brother!

However, our coins still carry a relic of the older American principle: "In God We Trust." This means that we do *not* trust in Washington, D.C., and its uncivil servants. Wisdom comes not from the White House, the Supreme Court, or the IRS, but from Almighty God, and to put our trust in men is dangerous, and it is sin.

Bureaucrats are very good at increasing their powers, not our freedom. Isn't it time we told our politicians that our trust is in God, rather than in them? Then our freedoms, instead of diminishing, would flourish.

Long ago, the prophet Isaiah declared: "Cease ye from man, whose breath is in his nostrils: for wherein is he to be accounted of?" (Isa. 2:22). If we are not partisans of freedom, then our faith will be in slavery.

★ *two* ★

DO WE MAKE TOO MUCH OF OUR PRESIDENTS?

WHEN THOMAS JEFFERSON was inaugurated as president, it was a simple and brief act before a few people. When it was over, Jefferson walked back to his boarding house. Dinner was already served, every seat was taken, and the newly inaugurated president had to wait for a place at the table. The same thing happened to President John Quincy Adams some years later. On a coastal sailing vessel, Adams was slightly late and had to wait his turn to eat.

In those days, a president was "no big deal." The federal government was small and insignificant, and the same was true of state, country, and city levels of civil government. Being president was not too important a position, nor was holding congressional office.

In fact, the last thing Americans wanted in those days was an important and powerful federal government. Even as late as the early 1900s, when the federal government was much larger than in Jefferson's day, it was still a minor factor in American life. During William Howard Taft's presidency, Washington, D.C., was still a small community with a handful of big buildings. In fact, the Tafts kept the family cow staked out in what is now the White House grounds but was then an open pasture.

What was important in those days was the American people. The people were the powers in the United States, and their faith and freedom made America great.

I submit that what you and I do, and other men like us do, is more important to the future of this country than what the White House and Congress do.

In the days of Jefferson and Adams, the people were not controlled, but the federal government was. The whole point of the Constitution was to handcuff the federal government and keep the people free. Today, the courts have reversed that. They have re-interpreted the Constitution to handcuff the people and to free the federal government from controls.

It is a serious mistake to look to the federal or state governments for our freedom. After all, if we gain power and freedom, they lose it. Many of our presidents, senators, and congressmen have been—and are—fine men. It is more important, however, for people to be godly and of a strong, sound character. We cannot vote in men and expect them to make this country strong when we ourselves refuse to be strong and self-reliant.

Thus, we do have a problem today: a much too strong federal government and an all too weak a people. If this continues, we will be a slave people at home and an oppressed people abroad.

Freedom begins in your life and mine, in our faith and character. We make too much of our presidents and far too little of ourselves. Most of all, we make too little of our sovereign Lord and God, and the result is that He is making little of us.

★ *three* ★

WHAT IS GOVERNMENT?

ONE OF THE more abused words in all languages today is *government*. When most people say *government*, they mean the federal government, or the state, county, or city governments, or all of them combined. Such use of the word is a major departure from Biblical, Puritan, and early American usage.

The Bible speaks of government as the attribute of God and of Christ. Isaiah 9:6 declares of the Messiah: "[T]he government shall be upon his shoulder."

On the human level, all government is by delegation from God, and there are seven basic levels of government. The *first* area — and the most basic — is self-government: the self-government of godly men. Without this, we have only lawlessness. One of our most serious problems today is lack of self-government.

The *second* area is the family. In the Bible, the family is set forth as the most important single "institution" or agency on earth. The family is man's first and most basic government, school, and church, from childhood on. If family government is weak, the country is weak.

A *third* area is the church. Too often today, the church either does not govern, or governs weakly, because people are in rebellion against all good government.

A *fourth* area is the school. For better or worse, schools are a very important form of government. Their influence as a form of government marks us all for life. Bad government in schools can — and usually does — mean bad government after schooling and for life.

A *fifth* area is our vocation—our work. You and I are governed by the work we do. It sets the pattern for our time use, our training, our income, and our daily lives. Our employers govern us, and the kind of work we do governs us. Our work is thus a very major form of government.

The *sixth* form is our community or society. What people think, do, and expect governs all of us. We feel social pressures which govern us.

Finally, a *seventh* form of government is civil government. There was a time when no one spoke of government as anything but *civil* government, one form of government among many. Today, civil government tries to control all other areas of government, by usurping the powers of self-government, family, church, school, work, and society. This is the meaning of totalitarianism: the control of all other forms of government by civil government. It spells certain disaster for any country.

What is government? It is certainly not the federal government. Over all, it is the government of Almighty God, and subject to God-ordained spheres of life and agencies. It begins with our own self-government.

If we deny the government of Almighty God, and if we fail in self-government, then we invite slavery and totalitarianism. You will get the kind of government you exercise.

★ *four* ★

IS THERE A WAR AGAINST THE FAMILY?

ALL OF US assume that we know what a family is, and that there can be no argument about its definition. After all, we grow up and live in a family; few things are more familiar to us.

However, the family has been the target of a very serious redefinition by federal agencies, one of the most radical and revolutionary changes in the history of the family. According to these peoples, there are two kinds of families. The "new" family is the "voluntary" family, whereas the older, traditional form is the "coercive" family.

It is important for us to understand what these terms mean. The "voluntary" family is seen as any association in a common dwelling of two or more homosexuals or lesbians. It can also mean a sexual commune, or a couple living together, or a group of runaway youth. Such a family is regarded as having moral stature because it is a free or voluntary association, not a compulsory or necessary one. We are told that the "voluntary" family must be granted legal status and protection.

The other kind of family, we are told, is the traditional (or Biblical family) pattern. This is called coercive, and thus, by implication, downgraded. The family members in the traditional family are supposedly not free, or are less free than those in the "voluntary" family, and hence not as socially advanced. Some have advocated as a "right" for children the "freedom" to move out and choose their own home.

Now the so-called "voluntary" family is really an antifamily group, a part of the war *against* the family. Someone once said that fascism would come in the name of antifascism. We can add that the planned destruction of the family is coming in the name of the family—the "voluntary" family.

The Biblical family pattern, however, is basic to the life of man, to his mental, emotional, and moral stability. To weaken the family is to weaken man and civilization. Carle C. Zimmerman, a Harvard sociologist, in his study of *Family and Civilization*, showed that the rise and fall of the stability and centrality of the family is basic to the rise and fall of civilization. Zimmerman showed how disastrous it has been, again and again, to replace the family's role in the life of man with an emphasis on lawless sex. When men trust in sex as the marital and psychological cure-all, they do major damage both to the person and to the family. They also produce a moral anarchism.

Zimmerman, in *The Family of Tomorrow*, referred to a common theme in novels; this theme is, "why did the world have to wreck my life?" The truer question is, of course: "Why did I wreck my life?" What right do I have to revolutionize the world, and the family, because I am a failure?

The failures of our day see themselves as an avant-garde, whose duty it is to change the world and make all things over in terms of their own sins. As a result, we have a war against the family, and we had better know it. Our future is at stake.

★ *five* ★

ARE NINE OUT OF TEN PROFESSORS UNFIT?

THE NEWSPAPERS CARRIED a front-page story entitled, “1 out of 10 Physicians May be Unfit.” According to the article, which quoted a Harvard professor of psychiatry, one out of ten may be alcoholic, addicted to drugs, or senile.

Pardon me if I take these statistics with a grain of salt. In fact, let me turn them around a bit. Nine out of ten psychiatrists may be unfit, judging by some evaluations. Certainly, some studies clearly show that a person’s chances of recovery are greater if he never visits a psychiatrist.

Let us go one step further. Some years ago, I studied at one of the world’s most important universities, both as an undergraduate and as a graduate student. I studied under some of the greatest scholars of the century, and I am grateful for what I gained from them. However, I believe I am being generous when I say that nine out of ten were very poor teachers, and seven out of nine were unfit to teach.

However, we have been looking into fields which are fairly good. How about the bureaucracy? I believe it would be generous to say that nine out of ten bureaucrats are unfit. Rather, we would have to say that very few of them are worth anything!

I am not trying to be cynical, but merely realistic and honest. An engineer in an aerospace plant once told me that nine out of ten engineers were paper shufflers and odd-jobs men, but it was the tenth man who had the ability and who created the jobs for all the others. In other words, talent and ability are limited, and in scarce supply.

We are told that Queen Victoria once complained to Prime Minister Gladstone that there were not many good preachers in the Church of England, and she wanted to hear more good pulpiteers. "Madam," said the Prime Minister, "there are not many good anything!" He was, of course, right.

There is another angle to this problem. Who determines who is good? Do we set up a bureaucracy in every area to pass judgment and to separate the good from the bad? We have, historically, had a very simple way of eliminating the poorer men. Its name is freedom of choice. If I do not feel that a doctor is qualified, I do not go to him. If the plumber's work is poor, I call another plumber the next time. We make the decisions. Since we are the people to be served, the right of decision belongs to us.

If we allow a committee unrelated to us, or a bureaucracy, to determine fitness, we then surrender a basic power over our lives into their hands. They can then finally say, as was done in the Soviet Union, that we are unfit to be free—or even unfit to live. I had an argument with a man on this subject, and he lost his temper and told me I was unfit to live. He meant it, too.

One final word. We have many self-promoting experts who tell us which and how many people are unfit for freedom. This, of course, is what they are really saying when they give us their "expert" opinions: they distrust freedom for anyone except themselves.

★ *six* ★

IS THERE A WAR AGAINST CHILDREN?

THE SWEDISH PARLIAMENT passed a law limiting the powers of parents in the name of children's "rights." Parents may not discipline their children either by physical spanking, or by depriving them of TV, or in any similar way imposing a restraint upon them.

The United Nations also has a child rights declaration, which makes the following points. *First,* the child must have reproductive freedom, that is, freedom for abortions, test-tube babies, and so on. *Second,* the child must have freedom for unrestrained sexual practices or preferences, including homosexual relations. *Third,* children must receive unisex education. *Fourth,* member states must provide federally-funded child development centers. *Fifth,* the child must have freedom from parental authority. *Sixth,* children must have "liberation" from patriotism and all such teaching; *seventh,* "liberation" from capitalism, and freedom for a new order, international and socialistic; *eighth,* "liberation" from religious training.

These so-called rights are being enacted piecemeal by various U.S. states and courts. In one state, the age of consent was lowered to thirteen. In many other states, teenagers may obtain abortions without parental knowledge or consent. The U.S. Supreme Court has sustained such laws. In one state, a minister was convicted of child-abuse for making his fourteen-year-old daughter attend Sunday school and church and sit through family prayers.

Much more can be added, but this is enough to indicate that a war is being waged against the Biblical family, and against children. It is a war which threatens to reach into your own home and family. Like it or not, you are involved.

According to the Bible, the care and discipline of children belongs to the family under God. From beginning to end, the Bible is full of commandments to parents and children, and the pattern for family life is to be derived from God, not from humanism or the state. What we are witnessing is a total war against Biblical faith, the family, and the child. Make no mistake about it; this is a religious war: humanism against Christianity. The lives of your children are at stake.

The courts and judges are saying that they, not the parents, will make the basic decisions concerning the child. Sociologists and legislators, together with the bureaucrats, claim that they know best what is good for our children, and they are sure that we parents are not good for them. In fact, some of them regard us as the worst possible guides for children. They seem sure that all wisdom and all light was born with them and their kind.

Clearly, there is a war against children and parents also. There is no escaping from this war, and there are no neutrals. Our future is at stake. Either we restore the family under God, or we lose our families and our freedom.

★ *seven* ★

ARE THE STATE SCHOOLS TEACHING RELIGION?

ONE OF THE things forbidden by the First Amendment is an establishment of religion, that is, tax funds going for the maintenance, support, or propagation of any one church group or religion, or any group of such churches. Today we see this principle routinely violated by the curriculum-makers of public education, or, more accurately, statist education. These curriculum-makers routinely make humanism and its values basic to their guidelines and texts.

I have many such guidelines and textbooks before me, but let me cite one as an example. Donald A. Read and Sidney B. Simon edited the *Humanistic Education Sourcebook* (1975) a textbook for teachers. One chapter is on "Values and Valuing." It is taken from a study of *Values and Teaching* by Louis E. Rath, Merrill Harmin, and Sidney B. Simon (1966). For them, a value cannot be derived from God — it has to be the free choice of the individual made from among many alternatives.

According to the authors, values are personal, not religious. Values are mainly a product of our experiences, "not just a matter of good and evil." Values come out of the flux of life, thus quite obviously not from God. We are told that parents should not tell children, "You shouldn't do that," or, "you shouldn't be interested in things like that." Whatever comes out of a child's experience is consistent with his life, and therefore his values. We cannot ask the child to deny his life and his values, say the authors, without asking him to be a hypocrite. Values are personal, they say, and respect for a person's life means respect for his experiences and values.

Given this standard of values, we would have to say that the values of Hitler, Stalin, and Jack the Ripper should have been respected. Some humanists would object that the values of these men had social consequences, but we must point out that since the people are persons, what is personal is also social or interpersonal.

The point is that a totally religious value system (for humanism is a religion according to the Supreme Court) is all too commonly taught in our state. This is an anti-Biblical religion which is contrary to the faith of most of us. On top of that, it is an established religion: public funds go to teach and propagate humanism. It is taught as "necessary." In Read and Simon's textbook, one chapter is entitled, "Humanism: Capstone of an Educated Person." In other words, without humanism, your education is incomplete and sadly defective.

The Bible and prayer have been banned from state schools, but humanism and its value system is openly taught. The First Amendment ban is applied only to Christianity and definitely not to humanism. This alien cult is accorded a privileged status at the expense of the rest of us. If you protest this, you are called a bigot. The day of newspeak and doublethink has come.

★ *eight* ★

ARE YOU A HUMAN BEING?

THE QUESTION, "ARE you a human being," may sound facetious and trifling, but it is less so when we read what some scientists are saying. For instance, Nobel Laureate Sir Francis Crick said, "No new-born baby should be declared human until is has passed certain tests regarding its genetic endowments and . . . if it fails these tests it forfeits the right to live." Another Nobel Laureate, Linus Pauling, wants to see every person's genotype tattooed on their forehead.

Now, if you and I ever made statements remotely approaching these in their moral madness, we would be shunned by all sensible people. However, when Nobel Prize winners make them, they are published and serious attention is given to their remarks.

In all this a monstrous evil is apparent. These scientists see man as simply another laboratory animal or guinea pig for experimentation. As a matter of fact, human beings are used for experimentation, especially mental patients and some still-living aborted babies.

Think about it. If scientists can be so callous towards human beings, why should we expect better from street hoodlums, muggers, and criminals? Why should contempt for human life be morally wrong in a criminal and yet legitimate in a scientist? If something is legitimate for people at the top of any society, you can be sure that it will soon be practiced at the bottom.

A sad fact about this fallen world is that sickness is contagious in most cases, but good health is not. A man can catch a cold, the flu, and a variety of diseases from people around him, but he cannot catch good health. The same is true of evil principles and standards; they are highly contagious, because man is by nature given to evil, and he has a natural affinity for it.

Is the day coming when Sir Francis Crick's hope will be realized, and none of use will be declared human beings unless a scientific committee tells us that we qualify? The answer to that question is, very clearly, "yes"—that day is coming, as long as we continue our present course. Not until we return to a Biblical faith can we arrest that trend. If we do not believe that man is created in the image of God, and solely to be governed by God's law-word, then nothing can prevent our lives from being expendable. Then we are human beings only if some scientist says so.

But we are not the creatures of science and the scientists, but the creatures of Almighty God. He made us, and He governs us. He defines us, and no man has the right to challenge His definition. If men dare to challenge God's definition of man, they will pay a price for it. No man has the right to deny the status of "man" to any other human being. *It is God-given.*

★ *nine* ★

ARE PARENTS BEING ABUSED?

WE HEAR A great deal these days about child abuse, but much too little (or nothing at all) about parental abuse. Make no mistake about it: parents are abused.

About a century ago, psychologists, psychiatrists, and psychoanalysts began providing everyone who messed up his or her life with a very convenient excuse: my parents did it do me. Granted, more than a few parents are very poor parents, but the foundation of all sound moral systems is that whatever others may do to us, or for us, we are personally responsible for what we are and do. An excuse, however, was provided by these men: my parents did it do me.

Some educators (not all) got into the act. Their excuse for failure was the family — the parents. Is Johnny doing badly, or is he a problem at school? Don't blame Johnny! Blame his parents. They are doing too much, or too little — whichever it is, they are all wrong.

Sociologists, child-welfare workers, and the courts got into the act. One idiot judge once remarked that there is no such thing as a bad child, only bad families. In other words, no one is a sinner, and all children are dear, angelic innocents until they grow up and become parents. Then, suddenly, they are the root of all evil!

Parents are so abused today that we can be grateful that a strong natural urge impels people to marry and to have children. Otherwise, with all the abuse parents get, it would be an unpopular calling.

On top of that, our courts are beginning to side with children in some very ugly situations. If you strike your child with just cause, to chastise him, you can be in serious trouble if he files a complaint against you. Some school counselors urge such children to file a complaint. However, if your child defies you and strikes you savagely, the welfare workers, counselors, or courts may well side with the child.

Parents are abused on all sides, and their love and work is underrated. No one but a father or a mother has the patience and love which rearing a child requires. There is no healthier environment for any child than the family, with its parental love and patience. Again and again, when God in the Bible wants to tell His people how great His love for and patience with them is, He compares Himself to a husband—or to a father and mother. God's images of His love are drawn from family life.

All this abuse of parents is a deadly evil. It is destroying the very foundations of life, and it is creating social conflict and disorientation to an unequalled degree. When the Ten Commandments call for honoring one's father and mother, the promise for obedience is a long and good life for individuals and nations. In other words, parental abuse is a ticket to a short life for men and nations, and for a civilization.

But what are we doing? In many states, there are legal efforts under way in the courts to remove the Ten Commandments from public buildings, courtrooms, and classrooms.

★ *ten* ★

DOES FREEDOM WORK?

ONE OF THE important aspects of American history was the original intention to establish a country in which the basic governing principle would be freedom. The Founding Fathers were aware that their beginning was far from perfect, and they were unhappy at having to compromise with slavery. They wrote in the abolition of the slave trade and expected slavery itself to disappear before too long.

There were other problems, of course, and American history has been anything but trouble-free. To depend on freedom as the solution can be slow at times. It means that people must learn and apply the answers, rather than having them applied from the top. It means, too, that evils sometimes linger longer than we would wish. However, the expectation was that problems could be best solved by a free people rather than by a powerful monarch, ruler, or bureaucracy.

This reliance on freedom as the basic instrument of government made the United States the envy of the world. Immigrants poured in from all over the world, and they continue to come in, because this seemed to be the land of opportunity, the land of freedom. By World War I, the United States was the envy of the world, and the dream country for many peoples. Travelers found that, even in very remote countries and places, people had some knowledge of America as a golden place.

Since then, of course, that dream has tarnished. Our follies have made us unpopular, and even hated.

Here at home, our belief in the governing value of freedom has been steadily replaced by a belief in control by the federal government and its bureaucrats. Some years ago, Lin Yutang wrote that, before he came to the United States, what it meant to him was Patrick Henry's great declaration, "Give me liberty, or give me death." On coming to this country, he found that we now had another slogan, "Give me security, or give me death." Of course, the ultimate security system is slavery.

Freedom did not fail; we failed. Freedom requires work, character, and responsibility, whereas a security system requires a slave master and a slave state. An old American principle was that eternal vigilance is the price of liberty. That statement came originally from famed Irish orator and leader John Philpot Curran (1750–1870), who, in a speech of 1790, said:

> It is the common fate of the indolent to see their rights become a prey to the active. The condition upon which God hath given liberty to man is eternal vigilance; which condition if he break, servitude is at once the consequence of his crime and the punishment of his guilt.

Few have said it as well as Curran. He was right: the choice is freedom or slavery. Either we make freedom (and the responsibility it involves) our way of life, or we be enslaved to an all-powerful and totalitarian state.

In more than one country in Europe, various forms of social security are bankrupting the nation while increasing the powers of the state. No politician dares call a halt to this insanity, and these nations stumble from crisis to crisis. Will this soon be said of us?

★ *eleven* ★

WHATEVER HAPPENED TO LOVE DAYS?

WHAT ARE LOVE days? They certainly were not hippie love-ins nor anything modern. Love days disappeared some years ago, to be replaced by something which is far from good. Love days used to go by a number of different names, depending on the region or the country. "Love days" is the English term; each language in Europe had its own, wherever the practice occurred.

Love days were a means of settling quarrels and disputes between people without going to court. They were once common in village and country life. In some areas, the law required people to observe love days. Disagreeing parties were required to come together in a public place, air their grievances publicly, and then settle them, sometimes with the help of a person known as the *oddwoman*, a woman whose work it was to arbitrate such conflicts.

In some centuries, the community required it. If either party expected anyone to have anything to do with them, they had to settle their differences. On market day, the two quarreling parties were required to lock arms and walk up and down the entire marketplace, chatting as friends all the while. It was the community's way of showing that all such conflict was deadly to the community and had to be resolved. Instead of aggravating the conflict, the community moved to resolve it and to deny to people the luxury of creating dissension.

We need love days now. If people quarrel, instead of others working to bring peace, others take sides and broaden the quarrel. They get on the telephone to gossip about the trouble and to fan the flames of dissension. We have become an extremely litigious people, and all too many such disagreements wind up in the courts.

All this says that we do not believe in a free solution, only a coercive one. When we bring in the state as a referee, we confess our inability (or our unwillingness) to resolve the matter in freedom. The situation is equally bad if we do not go to court, as we then prefer a permanent quarrel to peaceful relations.

Some forms of the love days had a requirement by law that people resolve their problems. Many did not—it was the moral force of community which required it, not the state. They believed in the words of St. Paul: "[B]e of one mind, live in peace; and the God of love and peace shall be with you" (2 Cor. 13:11).

The next time you hear about a conflict or quarrel in the community, remember this: by your retelling of the story—or your relish in gossip—you can make a trouble-day (or even a war-day) out of it. However, if you refuse to fuel the conflict and instead call for a peaceful and godly solution, you can help restore love days, and also restore the work of freedom to human relations.

★ *twelve* ★

WHAT IS THE PURPOSE OF TAXATION?

MOST OF US, while we may complain about taxes, rarely doubt the purpose of taxes. Most people will say that we must be taxed in order to support the various branches of civil government. This is what we were taught in school, and, like some other things we were taught, it is wrong. It may have been true at one time, but it is increasingly false.

L. L. Fuller, in his Storrs Lectures on Jurisprudence at Yale Law School, published in 1964, noted that even then the purpose of taxation had shifted (*The Morality of Law,* 166). Taxes have become a means of social control. They are used to control business and the business cycle. The allocation of economic resources is governed by taxation. Women are taxed by means of a high tax on all cosmetics, so that a substantial amount of the price women pay to enhance their appearance is a tax on a woman's desire to be beautiful. Taxes are used to identify professional gamblers and to make people pay for the use of alcohol. Travel is discouraged by high taxes on every kind of transportation, from the gas pump, to the cost of an automobile, to the price of a plane ticket. Taxes are often imposed for no other reason than to increase the power of the federal government.

We are taxed because we are alive; we are taxed when we die. As I warned my wife, "Neither of us can afford to die right now."

But this is not all. Professor Fuller says of the taxpayer: "May he not ask himself what, after all, is the difference between a tax and a fine? His mood of quiet desperation is not likely to be improved if he is unfortunate enough to learn that a famous justice of the Supreme Court of the United States used to insist that there is no difference" (166b). In other words, we are being fined for being alive!

In brief, the purpose of taxation is increasingly to limit self-determination. Taxes work deliberately to limit your freedom. Taxes, which began as a means of supporting the government, are used to limit our self-support.

We are justified in saying that, if there is no difference between a tax and a fine, then taxation has become immoral. We are therefore taxing (because of this view of taxation) the good citizen more heavily than the poor or bad citizen. We are fining success as much or more than we fine criminality. Is it any wonder that people are bitter and cynical about politics and politicians?

Most Americans love their country and would like to be proud of it once again, not disgusted nor ashamed. But what else can be expected when we are more tender to our enemies than we are to our own people? All too often, it seems as though our federal government has declared war against we the people, and taxation is its nuclear weapon to blast us with. How long can freedom survive in such a situation?

★ *thirteen* ★

DO OUR JUDGES MAKE SENSE?

IN NOVEMBER 1980, the *Washington Monthly* called attention to the growing irrationality of many court decisions. For example, the U.S. Court of Appeals recently ruled that the police can search a paper bag without a warrant, but a zippered leather pouch cannot be searched without a warrant.

The U.S. Supreme Court has given a series of strange decisions regarding aid to parochial schools. According to these decisions, tax funds can be used to supply textbooks to parochial school students but not to parochial schools. However, projectors and maps cannot be supplied at all, and guidance services cannot be on school grounds. All this is supposedly in the name of the First Amendment. Why are maps a violation of the First Amendment and textbooks are not? Do the judges know something about textbooks and maps of which the rest of us are ignorant?

In a Kansas City case, a civil servant was operating a private business on government time and with a government secretary to do it. The man's defense was that this was routine practice among federal officials. A jury found him guilty, and he resigned. The judge, however, soon thereafter overturned the jury verdict on the grounds that criminal intent was lacking. The civil servant then asked the Merit Systems Protection Board to reinstate him. An administrative judge not only ordered his reinstatement but also stipulated that the man was to be awarded $20,000 in back pay. The man, by the way, not only pleaded in his trial that everybody was doing it, but also that his job did not take much time so he used the vacant time for his own business.

The law and its judges cannot command respect if decisions, as well as laws, are irrational, unreasonable, and unfair. When the law and the courts make a judgment, it is necessary for that judgment to be right and just to the people if law enforcement is to flourish. However, when people weigh the law and the courts in the balances of justice and find them wanting, there will be serious unrest in a society.

Daniel tells us that the fingers of a man's hand appeared on the wall of Belshazzar's palace to write a sentence of final judgment, "*mene, mene, tekel, upharsin*," that is, a judgment stating that Babylon's day were numbered, it was weighed, and judged (Dan. 5:25–29). Now, increasingly, that same judgment is being written on the minds of many Americans as they see the directions of our laws and our courts.

The foundation of freedom is righteousness — or justice. If the law begins to represent instead a form of injustice or unrighteousness, the law itself will be judged by both God and man. Solomon said, "Righteousness (or justice) exalteth a nation: but sin is a reproach to any people" (Prov. 14:34). Today, all too often, our laws and courts are a reproach and an embarrassment to us. They have parted company with justice. They are instruments, too often, of injustice and power, not of justice and freedom.

★ SERIES FOUR ★

★ *one* ★

IS THE BED OF PROCRUSTES BACK AGAIN?

WHAT IS SAKE, and how do you classify it? Sake is a Japanese drink, and while I am not interested in sake, I am interested in freedom. The problem is this: sake does not fit the American definitions of either beer or wine. Beer is made from grain and wine from fruit. This should make sake a beer, but its alcohol content is that of wine.

Because California is a major rice producer, and because sake is made out of rice, a company was established to make sake, and there the trouble began. The federal government classified the Numano Sake Company as a brewery, but the state of California classified it as a winery. If the company met the classification of one, it would not satisfy the regulations of the other, so that to satisfy one branch of civil government meant being shut down by the other.

Finally, an awkward solution or compromise was reached; after all, both state and federal governments want the tax money. The basic issue remains, however.

The issue is this: remember the story from ancient Greece about a deadly innkeeper named Procrustes? Procrustes required all travelers to fit his bed. If they were too short, he and his men stretched them to fit; if they were too long, they cut off their feet. As a result, everyone who stopped to spend a night at the inn died in the bed of Procrustes.

Now, I submit that our state and federal agencies are the modern beds of Procrustes. We are required to fit their specifications and regulations, and if we do not fit, we are a target of hostile action.

If our civil governments are to be servants of the people, why do we have to meet their specifications? How can they serve us by compelling us to meet absurd regulations? What justice is there in trying to shut down a church, for example, because its ceiling is less than an inch short of the height required by a local building code? Very plainly, the bed of Procrustes is with us still.

For example, when is a church not a church? Does it cease to be a church and become a school when it has a Sunday school? Does a weekday parochial or Christian day school make it no longer a church but a school? Or is it a child-care facility, as the welfare officers of at least one state tried to say? In other words, the church feels it is in all these things still a church, but both the departments of education and of welfare claim jurisdiction, and each has its own, conflicting regulations.

The bed of Procrustes is an ancient myth, but it is also a very present reality.

★ *two* ★

DO YOU SLEEP BETTER AT NIGHTS BECAUSE OF THE BUREAUCRACY?

DO YOU SLEEP better at night, knowing that there are millions upon millions of bureaucrats trying to run your life, or does it give you nightmares? Do you try to avoid thinking about it?

The bureaucrats have a solution — and a regulation — for everything, and they seem to believe that they can do no wrong. Also, they seem to have no sense of humor.

A western ranch started operating a small guest-ranch some years back. Their help amounted to one couple: the wife did the cooking, and the man took care of the horses and rides into the mountains with the guests. There was a small cabin facility for the couple. The bureaucrats, however, interfered. Separate restroom facilities for male and female employees were required by their regulations; the fact that the couple was married and only hired married couples, made no difference.

Consider this case. The Vern Sprock family developed the Sierra Ski Ranch near Echo Summitt on U.S. Highway 50 in California. They built a day lodge on top of the mountains. It is a very modern structure, with alternate energy sources: solar heating panels and a windmill-powered generator. State bureaucrats, however, made them add two wheelchair toilets, although the lodge can only be reached by skiing (*Inquiry*, December 8, 1980, 2)!

Bureaucrats regard their regulations like the law of the Medes and the Persians: beyond appeal or exception, an infallible and all-wise regulation in every cases. In other words, implicit in all such instances is a belief in bureaucratic infallibility.

Now, I do believe that God is infallible and that His law is true and righteous altogether. Precisely for that very reason, I am dubious about man's law. After all, man is a sinner; man can be and always is highly fallible, very prone to error, and all too inclined to believe that his foolishness is wisdom.

This is why I believe that we dare not trust any man, or any institution, with too much power. Such a distrust of man was once the American view of civil government. Now, however, too many people are confusing the federal government with God. The result is a growing disaster.

However, it is the Lord who is my Shepherd, not Big Brother in Washington. We are much safer living in terms of "In God We Trust" than in terms of a trust and faith in the federal government and its bureaucracy. We are in trouble because we have expected more from the federal government than from God, and so we are getting disasters from Washington and judgments from God. Are you sleeping any better at night because of the bureaucrats?

It is time for us to rethink our faith—and our foundations. For too long we have lived as though the only true God were the federal government, only to find increasingly that it has clay feet and is a dangerous idol.

★ *three* ★

HOW MUCH HONESTY IS THERE IN CIVIL GOVERNMENT?

THE YEAR 1980 was an interesting one: more Congressmen were convicted than members of the Mafia, perhaps, and more than a few evidences of dishonesty in high places were revealed.

There was, however, one bit of good news from, of all places, the Internal Revenue Service! Not many of us have a good word for the IRS, but this audit does deserve one. The results were very interesting. The IRS selected 168 of its own auditors for audit; the choice was a random selection. There were serious errors in half of these returns. Of those in error, forty-two of the auditors had underpaid their income tax by an average of $720. The general public's underpayment is approximately half that amount, at $340 (*Inquiry*, December 8, 1980, 2).

Now, this raises a very interesting moral problem. If a watchman is less honest than the people he is watching, then he is not much of a watchman! Most federal agencies are almost certainly by no means as efficient as the IRS. If these agencies are more wasteful (and data reveals that they are) and less honest (and the evidence indicates this is so) than the general public, then we are not only badly governed but also wrongly governed.

After all, we do have a right to expect our police to be more honest than the criminals, our clergymen to be more godly and obedient to the Lord than the flock, and federal officials to be more honest than the public. The old line is still true: Caesar's wife must be above reproach, and so, too, must be Caesar and Caesar's assistants. If they are not, then cynicism and bitterness quickly infect the people.

At one time, the idea was commonplace that the function of civil government is to be an umpire or referee, not taking sides but administering even-handed justice. Now, federal and state governments and agencies have become the rule-makers, coaches, players, and manipulators. They are no longer like arbitrators in a game — they own and control the game!

The result is social disorder. Our present scene is marked by distrust and cynicism. In recent years, one president campaigned for office on the promise of bringing us together, only to divide us all the more. No party or man can bring us together, especially not when no one shows any trust in man — nor can one with any common sense.

Our old motto, which is still on our coins, is, "In God We Trust." This means in God, not politicians, the federal government, the president, or the bureaucracy. When we trust in God, we ourselves will become more trustworthy to the degree that we obey Him and order our lives in terms of His Word. "Except the Lord build the house, they labor in vain that build it," is an ancient and tried truth and wisdom. We need to rebuild in terms of it.

★ *four* ★

IS CIVIL GOVERNMENT COSTING US TOO MUCH?

DURING 1980, THE total cost to us for federal, state, and local units of civil government was close to one trillion dollars. The nonpartisan Tax Foundation estimated it to be $926.7 billion. This means, as *U.S. News and World Report* calculated, a cost to each American household of $11,715.00.

If you wondered why your income is not going too far these days, these figures give you the reason. Of course, not all of that $11,715 came out of your income in direct taxation, but you are paying for it one way or another. Some of that money was the result of federal, state, or local borrowings which you will pay for eventually.

Moreover, it is a mistake to assume that much of these tax funds came from taxes on corporations and businesses. The people pay all taxes. Any tax on gasoline, an automobile, a refrigerator, or anything else is simply added to the price of the merchandise and passed on to us. Since the manufacturers' total profits are something like 3 to 5 percent per unit, they cannot afford to pay the taxes unless they are passed on to the consumer.

The result is inflation. Inflation is a made-in-Washington product. It is popular with politicians to blame inflation on capital and labor (or on the people), but it is a federally created product. In fact, almost the only thing the various national governments of the world do well these days is to create inflation, a highly undesirable product. Various economists will give us differing estimates on the inflation rate in 1980, from 12 to 16 percent. Unless you have a salary or income increase to match the rate of inflation, you are in trouble.

In fact, most of us are in trouble because of federally-created inflation. Inflation erodes confidence in civil government; it creates social unrest and decay. Inflation increases federal power and limits our freedom. In virtually every area of life, inflation exercises a deadly influence. Inflation can almost be compared to a terminal disease.

The cure for inflation is a moral as well as an economic one. Inflation is a form of legalized larceny. When a people have larceny in their hearts, they are ready to legalize it. When we as a people begin with a soak-the-rich demand, we soon want a soak-the-middle-class politics, and finally, a soak-the-poor and everybody else program. The result is the triumph of the politics of envy—and inflation.

There is a relationship between sound money and sound morality. Today, we have neither. We cannot have the one without the other. We cannot have a sound morality which asks others to pay the price for our moral concerns. Morality begins at home, in our own lives, not in our demands on others. The greatest price we are paying for inflation is a moral price.

★ *five* ★

IS SANITY TOO MUCH TO ASK FOR?

SOMETIMES, BECAUSE MY duties take me all over the country — and have for years — I miss reading the daily newspapers. As a result, I miss some news now and then. Somewhere along the line, I must have missed news of an important congressional act repealing sanity because there certainly seems to be more than a little hostility against it.

Take this, for example. In the January 1981 issue of *Harper's* magazine, Theodore Roszak calls attention to some prime examples of respectable insanity. One prominent psychotherapist told Roszak over lunch that people sleep and die only because they have been mistakenly programmed to believe they have to: reprogram people, he held, and you can eliminate sleep and death and chalk up a victory for therapeutics!

If this is psychotherapy, perhaps we are locking up the wrong people in our mental institutions.

Now, obviously God neither sleeps nor dies, but for man to suggest that we can do the same is to assume that man is a god who has not realized his potential. This is, of course, exactly what many people insist on declaring.

Now, if man does not know that he is a man, a creature made by God (not by himself), and a creature who is born and will also die, then man cannot face any problem intelligently or realistically.

If we begin with a false problem, we end up with false solutions. If we cannot face realistically some of the most elementary problems of human life, our lives are certainly headed for defeat, and our country too.

No one who lives in terms of illusions can long be free. I once met a man who was under the illusion that he was the wealthiest rancher in his area; actually, he had lost the little ranch he once owned. However, he believed that he had millions in the bank and regularly and generously wrote checks on his nonexistent account. What his checks bought him was a return to the state mental hospital.

There are, however, no mental hospitals for nations who live in terms of illusions. No one will take care of the United States in such case. The United States has fallen under the sway of messianic delusions of saving the world with dollars, guns, and diplomacy, and this delusion is destroying us. Any man who plays God winds up at best a fool, but more likely, in the scrapheap of life and history. We should not be surprised that the United States is governed by delusions, when a prominent psychotherapist thinks we can program men out of sleeping and dying, and when so many of us live daily in terms of false hopes and active delusions.

The world is not what we wish it might be, but what God makes it to be and what our sins and shortcomings have brought it to be. We cannot change the world until we begin to live in terms of reality—God's reality—not our illusions. Are you living in the world of soap operas—television-made or Washington-made—or in terms of God's order?

★ *six* ★

IS THE WAR ON CRIME A REAL WAR?

ONE OF THE most common of news stories today, all over the country, is about our supposed war on crime. State and federal officials are holding conferences and issuing press releases about their concern. One cynical police chief of one of our biggest cities came out of one such conference stating that the governor's interest in crime was limited to grabbing headlines, not helping the police.

With all our federal and state authorities supposedly marshalling their forces against crime, we would expect some decline in the crime rate. Instead, crime, next to civil government, is the biggest growth industry in America and all over the world.

The state and federal governments are, in fact, spending more time going after you and me than going after criminals. As a starter, consider all the effort spent in collecting and auditing tax returns.

Even more, state and federal agencies often spend more time and effort going after churches, Christian-school teachers, and Sunday-school teachers than after criminals. In one major state, the large attorney-general's staff is busy, not with the Mafia, but with Christian schools which exercised their free speech by speaking out on the issue of homosexuality. This supposedly made them "political" and hence not deserving of tax exemption.

The welfare officer of a major state has set forth a plan to license every Sunday school in the state as a child care facility if even one child is present without his or her parents. Furthermore, all fifty states are now developing child control programs, *not* for delinquent children, but for all children.

Is there a war against crime, or is there a war against we who are law-abiding and God-fearing citizens? More time, money, and energy is spent in people control than in crime control. The Mafia is putting money into the bank; we are withdrawing what little we have to pay taxes which will be used to control us.

One national magazine (*Inquiry*) recently expressed cynicism about the war on crime. The editor, who refuses to be identified with either the right or the left, simply stated his disbelief in the integrity of the statist claims saying, *"Power over the people, not service to the people or the cause of justice, has become the major concern of state and federal authorities."* The result is a steady decline in our freedom as the power state grows bigger and bigger at our expense.

The modern power state, all over the world, is rapidly becoming Public Enemy Number One. The United States, the Soviet Union, Red China, France, Britain, Italy, Germany, and other states everywhere may sometimes be at war with each other. More and more, however, it seems as though they are always at war against their own peoples. Modern man needs freedom from the power state.

★ *seven* ★

HAVE WE FORGOTTEN THE FUNDAMENTALS?

IN *Chronicles of Culture* (November–December 1980), Professor Thomas Molnar recounted the following recent events:

> Indira Gandhi, while exercising dictatorial powers . . . let her son deal with the problem of India's overpopulation by having police surround movie houses, collect the males, and transport them to sterilization centers. Some 10,000,000 Indians lost their capacity to reproduce. In Indonesia, West Sahara (Polisario), Iran, and Nicaragua, women gouged out prisoners' eyes, emasculated them, then gagged them with their genitals. (45)

These are grim and ugly facts, but increasingly commonplace all over the world.

When I was a schoolboy, I greatly enjoyed pirate tales like Robert Louis Stevenson's *Treasure Island.* I knew that such stories dealt with times long gone and had nothing to do with the present. Times have changed since then. Now, piracy is commonplace in the Caribbean Sea and in the East Indies. Small ships are regularly seized, and all who are aboard are murdered. Recently, a friend gave me a copy of his friend's logbook of an around-the-world voyage on a small yacht. It was a strange feeling to read in it the precautions to avoid pirates. The world is clearly slipping back into barbarism, not only on the high seas but on our city streets.

One writer recently called attention to the "chilling taste for violence." This love of violence is apparent among criminals and also among television and film viewers. So far-reaching is this taste for violence that simple matters of political protest have increasingly courted violent confrontations with fervor and delight.

Once, not too many years ago, we regarded violence and terrorism as a thing of the past. Hitler was dead, and Stalin too, and supposedly, the world was going to evolve to a higher moral level.

Quite obviously, we have lost our way, or perhaps we should say *the way*. Centuries ago, the psalmist said:

> Except the LORD build the house, they labour in vain that build it: except the LORD keep the city, the watchman waketh but in vain. (Ps. 127:1)

About fifty years ago, in *The Revolt of the Masses*, Jose Ortega y Gasset spoke of the new barbarians as scientists, specialists, and others who believe "that civilization is *there* in just the same way as the earth's crust and the forest primeval." In other words, the new barbarism assumes that twenty centuries of Christianity and its accomplishments are a *natural fact*, like the air we breathe, rather than a *moral and religious fact*. We are a part of the new barbarism if we forget that the fundamentals of our faith are also the fundamentals of our civilization.

Freedom is perishing because we are neglecting the foundations of freedom. The worldwide retreat into barbarism will not be solved by the politicians. It is a moral and a religious fact, and it calls for a moral and religious answer.

★ *eight* ★

WHAT IS THE COST OF CIVIL GOVERNMENT?

LET US LOOK again at some data I cited not too long ago. Recently, the *U.S. News and World Report* published some data on spending by federal, state, and local areas of civil government. The total for 1980 came close to a trillion dollars, or $926.7 billion. This represents a 12.6 percent increase in twelve months, and the amount will be greater in 1981. This statist spending came to about 40 percent of the total value of all the goods and services produced in the United States in 1980. If these outlays are divided by the number of families in the United States, it comes to $11,715 for each household.

This, however, is only the *financial* cost. The *economic* cost has been a steady stifling of the economy, so that we are less and less able to compete on world markets. American capital and labor once represented the world's most productive force. Now, saddled by the costs of big civil government, we are less and less competitive on the world markets.

There is also a *political* cost. When the power state of today controls 40 percent of the economic wealth annually, it is out of control. The power state controls the people, not the people the state. As a result, we see administrations change, but not the ongoing bureaucracy and its drive for more power.

There is also a *human* cost. More and more people are disillusioned with the political process and regard it as an empty façade for a power elite. People of varying political opinions have come to this conclusion.

Such a cynicism concerning the political process is a dangerous and potentially revolutionary fact.

There is also a *moral* cost. The more power and money that the state takes from us, the less responsibility we have and exercise. The result, then, is an erosion and a decline of freedom.

Obviously, we are paying too high a price for civil government. That price is more than money; it includes character and responsibility.

The solution to this problem involves a steady limitation of the proliferating bureaucracy of the power state. This, however, is not enough. What is even more necessary is the development of a character in us, the people, which is more congenial to freedom. We cannot criticize the subsidies others get without also criticizing our own. Someone in the John F. Kennedy administration, some years ago, very aptly described the critics of Washington, D.C. The typical critic went to public schools, riding in a county bus on a public highway; went to college on the GI bill, bought a house with an FHA loan, started a business with a loan from the Small Business Administration, made money, retired on social security, and then sat back to criticize the welfare program, demanding that the freeloaders be put to work.

In other words, if freedom and independence do not begin with us, we cannot demand them of other men. Freedom suffers, and a country declines in moral responsibility, if what we want from Washington, D.C., is a necessity and what others want is pork-barrel legislation.

★ *nine* ★

WHAT DOES LEGITIMATE MEAN?

WHEN WE TALK about stage plays in New York, London, or elsewhere, we speak of "the legitimate theatre." What does this term mean? Why should stage play be called "legitimate"?

This usage goes back to Shakespeare's day. Plays previously had been church-oriented miracle and morality plays. In the Elizabethan era, the theatre began to flourish at a remarkable rate. The royal government immediately stepped in to license and control the stage. Three theatres were licensed in London, Drury Lane, Covent Garden, and, in the summer only, the Haymarket. Any other performance was illegitimate. This law continued until 1843. Thus, the licensed and controlled theatres were called "legitimate theatre," a term we still use without realizing its meaning.

The legitimate theatre was a *controlled* theatre. We fail to realize how much propaganda there is in Shakespeare. His historical plays were written to glamorize the Tudor dynasty and to make legitimate by falsification the illegitimate seizure of power by Henry VII. Thus, for the Crown, the legitimate theatre served an illegitimate purpose.

As time passed, the theatre became more and more trifling as writers sought to avoid problems with the court. The comedy of manners, which concentrated on witty fluff, became paramount to the English state, together with operatic, heroic plays.

Why is all of this important to us? The point is that the English state was defining what was legitimate in the theatre. If Shakespeare had produced his plays on a bootlegged basis, would his work have been any less legitimate?

Now, the question is important for us, because, with federal grants and subsidies, we are quietly moving back towards a legitimate theatre, legitimate arts and sciences, and legitimate entertainment on television. It took more than two and a half centuries for England to escape from a "legitimate" theatre to a somewhat free theatre. Now we are moving into licensed theatre, entertainment, arts and sciences, and *education.* When government authority is believed to be the ultimate determiner, state-controlled and state-licensed schools are presumed to have legitimacy, even though Christian schools may be better.

In one area after another, a battle was waged in recent centuries against the idea that church or state had the right or ability to declare something legitimate or illegitimate and to exercise controls over it. The results of that battle were major advances in freedom. We are now acting as though that struggle was a mistake, as though a higher stage of progress requires such a surrender of freedom and choice. If we give the state the power to decide what is illegitimate or legitimate, that power state will eventually place freedom — and us — on the list of things illegitimate.

★ *ten* ★

HOW GOOD WERE THE GOOD OLD DAYS?

WE HEAR MORE than a little talk these days about urban pollution. The assumption in such discussions is that suddenly, with the automobile, our good, clean air was polluted. Now, granted, our air needs cleaning up, but was it clean before?

The horse, in the days before the automobile, was a remarkable polluter. In 1907, Milwaukee, for example, had 350,000 people; horses provided transportation, and they daily left 133 tons of manure on the streets. Horses brought food into the city, and these horses left their calling cards everywhere. In the summer, the carriage wheels quickly turned the manure into dust which floated in the air and into houses. If it rained when your wash was on the line, the manure dust in the air was drenched into your wash and ruined it. In the winter snows and rain, the manure was turned into a splashing slush which sometimes moved good people to profanity. In those days, a gentleman walked on the street-side of the sidewalk in order to protect his lady from the splash of the manure slush.

The manure carried disease, and a breeze would carry tetanus and other spores everywhere. These were the good old days of epidemics of cholera, dysentery, infant diarrhea, smallpox, yellow fever, and typhoid. The automobile does some polluting, but it helped eliminate these deadly pollutants.

Of course, the manure bred flies by the billions, and the sparrows multiplied into a national pest, feeding on manure. In those days, it was difficult to enjoy a shade tree on a hot summer day because of the sparrow droppings.

But this is not all. Horses were mistreated and regularly dropped dead in the streets. In 1880, for example, New York had 15,000 dead horses left on its streets; as late as 1912, Chicago had 10,000 dead horses in the year. There were no license plates on the horses, so the owners could not be traced. Before the dead horses could be removed, the neighborhood dogs feasted on them and dragged bits and pieces into alleyways and backyards.

In other words, the good old days were very polluted, and, to put it plainly, more than a little stinky. Now, I am all for good, clean air, but don't romanticize the past and don't overreact.

We do need laws to protect ourselves from pollution, but perfection does not come overnight. Moreover, while technology is sometimes the offender, it has more often than not been an advantage in cleaning up the air and environment. Used wisely, it can further the work of conservation.

In brief, if we have an unrealistic view of the past, we have an unrealistic view of the present. We then indulge in name-calling, not problem-solving. Instead of furthering progress and freedom, we hamper it.

★ *eleven* ★

WHAT'S WRONG WITH NOSTALGIA?

WHEN IT COMES to nostalgia, I plead not guilty. I want no part of it. I am sure there were a great many good things in the past, but I like today better, and I shall enjoy tomorrow even more. I know we live in troubled times, and I expect very serious troubles in the years just ahead, but I believe that God is on the throne of the Universe, and I like His government.

One of the things which irks me every winter is the happy and silly nostalgia about horse-drawn sleighs. At Christmas, we hear about sleigh bells in the snow. Usually some magazine will include a romantic painting about happy, singing people on a sleigh ride.

I visited somebody, who almost reverently showed me a recent buy — authentic sleigh bells.

Now, let me tell you the truth about sleighs. I know them firsthand from life in the high mountain country some years back. Sleighs are one of the most miserable ways to travel ever devised by man. Nothing can chill you more than a sleigh ride. You are open to the cold, freezing air, and it cuts you like a knife as you go dashing through the snow. You have a choice. If you go fast, the cold air cuts and chaps your face in a hurry and leaves you gasping for air, but the air is ice-cold, and your breath leaves little icicles on your nose and eyebrows. If you go slow, then in spite of all your clothes and robes, you turn slowly into a human icicle, numb and cold. There is no hearty "ho! ho! ho!" left in you.

But there is much worse. Dragging a sleigh through and over snow-covered roads and fields is particularly hard work for the horses. Among other things, it makes the horses very gassy. As you handle the reins, your nose is on the same level as and directly behind the horses' rear ends. I leave the rest to your tender imagination. The one question in your mind is this: will I die of asphyxiation, or will I freeze to death? There must be, you tell yourself, a less painful way to go.

No, not nostalgia for me. Give me a good, well-heated automobile to drive, with my wife by my side, and I feel far more romantic and much more a free man than I ever felt in an ice-cold sleigh with my nose under a horse's rear end! I like progress, and I want more of it. It gives me freedom, and I like freedom. I can feel very romantic about freedom. Freedom is the air I want to breathe.

This is why I prefer the present and the future to the past. I want to make the present more free, and the future a good and free one for my children and grandchildren. I cannot do so by perpetuating silly, romantic myths about the past. For all our problems today, the preferred world for me is the here and now. This is where I am alive.

★ *twelve* ★

ARE WE RUNNING OUT OF SPACE?

ON ALL SIDES today, we hear a great deal of talk about overpopulation. Such talk is not new. Not long after World War II, some so-called experts predicted that, by 1975, overpopulation would lead to massive and worldwide famines; a book was published to set down these forecasts. Others predicted that, by the end of the century — or by 2020 at the latest — there would be standing room only.

Is this true? The facts indicate that the world is really very much underpopulated and far from running out of space. Anyone traveling by air, over any continent, will see mostly empty spaces, some farmland, and here and there, human settlements.

In the United States only, 2 percent of all privately owned land is used for housing. Only 3 percent of all privately owned land is used for commercial, industrial, and recreational development. Remember, much of our country, especially in the West, is federally owned.

But this is not all. As more and more advances are made in farming, and productivity increases, the amount of land needed for farming decreases. Many farms in New England and the East have reverted to woodlands, and many Southern farms are now tree farms. The United States, on less and less land, not only feeds itself, but is a major source of food for the world.

Old Russia, under the tsars, was the breadbasket of Europe. Under the Soviet dictatorship, it became a major food buyer on the world market. Every decade, its food problems grew worse until there was a serious food shortage in the country.

More than a generation ago, E. Parmalee Prentice's studies showed that there is a close correlation between freedom and productivity. A free country is a productive country. It uses space more wisely, and it increases the utility and productivity of land and resources.

We are definitely not running out of space. We are, however, showing signs of running out of common sense. When we create imaginary problems, we cannot deal with our real ones. Ancient Greece talked about overpopulation in its last days, and so too did the dying Roman Empire. In both cases, the problem was a tyrant state which blamed its problems on the people, not on itself.

The idea of overpopulation is also a dangerously racist myth. If we say there are too many people, we will next say that there are too many people of some race or group we dislike. Such an assumption leads to ungodly and explosive social implications. We have seen, in recent years, abortions promoted among some minority groups. Such hatred is a threat to freedom and order.

We have enough problems today without creating or promoting imaginary ones. Land economist and statistician Homer Hoyt said, "Even in our most densely developed urban areas, there is more land than we will ever be able to use for housing, shopping, and industrial development."

It is time to junk imaginary problems and deal with the real ones.

★ *thirteen* ★

ARE WE MOVING INTO SLAVERY?

FROM 1854 TO 1884, Herbert Spencer wrote some essays later published under the title, *The Man Versus the State*. One of these essays was titled, "The Coming Slavery." Looking ahead to our century, Spencer foresaw the development of a new slavery. The old slavery was in process of being abolished all over the world. The old slavery was the private ownership of some men by other men. The new and coming slavery would be different and more deadly. It would be the ownership of the people by the state.

The roots of the new slavery, he said, would be in a supposedly humane belief. He saw the churches themselves falling prey to and advocating this dangerous premise. As Spencer stated it, "The current assumption is that there should be no suffering, and that society is to blame for that which exists." There were, thus, two aspects to this malignant and deadly belief.

First, the belief that there should be no suffering is a denial of the need to grow or to pay the penalty for sins and errors. Parents are commonly addicted to this error. They do not want their children to go through what they had to go through, with the net result that their children fail to develop the character their parents have. Apply this principle to society and you have social anarchy.

Second, there is the belief that society is to blame for that which exists. Responsibility and character, however, are primarily and essentially personal. When we deny that personal foundation of responsibility, we undermine both law and civilization.

When we make such deadly assumptions, namely, that there should be no suffering and that society is to blame for what exists, we then work to *regulate society*, not to develop character, knowledge, and abilities in the individual. The end result of these regulations, Spencer predicted, is more regulations, and, finally, mass enslavement. All of us then become, in effect, the prisoners of the state. The slave society has increasingly one answer to all problems: more regulations — or more slavery. Those who try to maintain their freedom begin to give up and begin to join the ranks of the slaves, and you have a revolution into slavery. As Spencer noted:

> To one who doubts whether such a revolution may be so reached, facts may be cited showing its likelihood. In Gaul, during the decline of the Roman Empire, "so numerous were the receivers in comparison with the payers, and so enormous the weight of taxation, that the labourers broke down, the plains became deserts, and wood grew where the plough had been." In like manner, when the French Revolution was approaching, the public burdens had become such, that many farms remained uncultivated and many were deserted: one quarter of the soil was absolutely lying waste; and in some provinces one-half was in health. (45)

Spencer's prediction was right. We are indeed moving into the new slavery. But responsibility is personal, and we are not helpless pawns. The time has come for us to move into freedom.

★ SERIES FIVE ★

★ *one* ★

CAN WE TRUST STATISTICS?

CAN WE TRUST the statistics issued by Washington, D.C., and its federal agencies? Some years ago, I knew a very successful corporate executive who told me that an important aspect of his success was his distrust of all federal statistics. Since his success depended on knowing what happened in his own field, he had men compiling statistics for him.

Too many of us have been brought up to believe naïvely in the validity of statistics. The problem with that is that statistics may be both accurate and misleading at one and the same time. For example, it can be demonstrated that a higher percentage of people who check into hospitals will die than do those who walk into bars. Does it follow, then, that hospitals are a more dangerous place than bars?

Now, that example is an obvious one. Let us consider another, not quite as obvious. A few years back, an article set forth statistics which supposedly proved that all adoptions through state agencies were far more successful and problem free than adoptions through all private agencies combined. These statistics showed a high ratio of serious problems developing among private agencies. However, on closer examination, the statistics, while accurate, were giving us a false and prejudiced picture of adoption agencies. The statisticians had classified adoptions sponsored by church agencies together with illegal and criminal-controlled adoptions! What they had avoided doing was to compare, say, church-sponsored adoptions with state-sponsored adoptions. Using the same data, if we compared all church-sponsored adoptions against all statist and criminal adoptions, the church agencies would clearly come out far ahead. Again, the statistics would be accurate, but the conclusion would again be misleading.

In other words, given a collection of statistics, how we classify and arrange them will determine what conclusion we get.

Now, our biggest and most impressive statistics-gathering agency is the federal government. Every federal agency, virtually, regards statistics as an important tool for making a case for its own worth, for claiming more powers, and for demanding more money. Not only do these agencies collect statistics to promote their own welfare, but they also create supposedly independent fact-finding agencies to provide them with more statistics to use on Congress and the people.

Thus, a key purpose of statistics is to increase the credibility and the powers of the bureaucracy at the cost of our freedom as a people. One important way of defending our liberties is to distrust these federal statisticians. They have an axe to grind, and they are using it against us.

★ *two* ★

DO WE HAVE A NEW KIND OF POLICE?

IN AN ARTICLE in *Reason* magazine (February, 1981), an Australian champion of civil liberties, Gary Sturgess, wrote on the growing menace of Australia's bureaucratic police. As more and more bureaucratic agencies control men and society, these agencies gain powers sometimes denied to the regular police. According to Sturgess, "The combined strength of Australia's police forces is now greater than that of the Australian army." Sturgess further points out that, in Queensland alone, there are now over 3,200 bureaucrats of the regular police. About 120 different kinds of inspectors have power of entry onto private property, and tens of thousands of officials other than the 3,200 can be granted like powers by senior officers in the bureaucracy.

These powers give the bureaucrats the right to enter, search, seize, arrest, and detain, and to destroy private property on suspicion, not on proof. One of the most disliked of these bureaucrats is the tax inspector, but many other bureaucrats rival him.

The regular police are restrained by the common law, so their powers remain the same as they were 150 years ago. These police powers are basically the same powers every citizen has. The problem in Australia is thus not with the regular police, but the new and growing bureaucratic police.

This problem, however, is *not* limited to Australia. It is also increasingly true of the United States. Although we are limiting the powers of our police in dealing with criminals, we are seeing a steady increase of the police powers of the bureaucracy in dealing with us. We have been downplaying the military power of the United States and its capacity to deal with foreign enemies. At the same time, however, we have limited the powers of the police in dealing with domestic enemies, or criminals. We have, however, been *increasing* the powers of the bureaucracy over us. In other words, the main target of repressive actions by state and federal governments is the law-abiding citizen.

As a result, our civil liberties are diminishing and are seriously threatened. This threat comes from state and federal agencies. Instead of being our protectors, they have become our controllers.

Sturgess writes, "The stage is set for totalitarian bureaucracy." Less and less does the new totalitarianism rely on a dictator. More and more, all over the world, the new totalitarianism is a rule by bureaucracies. The forms of representative government, with elections and legislative bodies, are retained, but the power is more and more in the hands of bureaucratic bodies. We are ruled, not by laws, but by executive orders and regulations. In all of this, the victim is freedom. Legislators come and go, but the bureaucracy remains. Either the bureaucracy goes, or freedom does.

★ *three* ★

IS IT HARD TO BE RICH?

A VERY SUPERIOR young man, worth a great many millions, told me not too long ago that it is not easy to be rich. A few years ago, I might have laughed at the idea, but not so any more.

I have not suddenly become rich, nor is there any likelihood of that happening. However, I have been mistaken for a rich man, with some interesting results. In the very recent past, our foundation was given some large, used, and expensive cars. The donors decided to switch to economy cars, and we got the big ones. One of these was a particularly expensive car, with all kinds of accessories. Driving it made me feel rich. Also, people took me for a rich man, although, all my life, I have never personally been able to drive more than an older used car.

The results were interesting, to say the least. As I stopped at a service station, or pulled up at a motel or hotel, people were ready to talk and wanted to know what line of work I was in. On an impulse, I gave, on different occasions, two different answers, *both true*. On some occasions, I said I was a writer, which I am, being the author of thirty or more books. At other times, I said that I am a minister, which is also true.

The reactions were very different. Those who saw me as a writer were ready to please me, flatter me, and also to tell me of foreign luxury cars I might like to try some time. Those who saw me as a minister were immediately hostile, angry, and very prone to nasty remarks! They obviously believed that it is necessary for a minister to be poor and in need of a hand-out.

But this was not all. Being taken for a rich man also means that one should be taken for all that can be had. People were immediately out to con me, to relieve me of some of my supposed riches. I found out that it is not easy to be rich, or to be taken for a rich man; people are envious and even hostile.

However, it is not easy to be in the middle class, nor to be poor. Our age promotes class conflict, envy, and hatred. Whatever you are, someone resents you and is out to exploit you, or to blame you for much of society's problems. In other words, where class conflict is promoted, everyone is the victim as well as the oppressor, and resentment is present on all sides.

A world of envy and class hatred is not an easy world to live in. Instead of increasing peace and freedom, it works to create conflict, and each group wants to hurt and cripple some other class. Each then sees its own freedom as necessitating the destruction of someone else's freedom. In a world of envy and hatred, it is hard to be rich, poor, or middle class, because all life is soured and tainted by class conflict. As a result, all suffer and freedom wanes. It is not easy to be anything in such a world. The truth still remains that we are required by God to love our neighbors as ourselves.

★ *four* ★

WHAT KIND OF ADVICE DO YOU WANT?

DO PEOPLE REALLY want advice when they ask for it? George Washington always refused to give advice, because he saw that people too commonly only wanted that counsel which would confirm their desires. Was he right?

When World War II ended, the United States asked the German generals for their advice. Had the World War II unified military command worked better than the previous divided command? Would it be wise, in other words, to drop the separate departments of the navy and of the army for a single command? All the German generals regarded the unified command as a disaster, and said so, except for one. That man, General Hans Guderian, for his own reasons (and partly his anti-Americanism), favored the single command. We adopted a unified command. The reason, of course, was that this was what we had wanted all along. All we wanted was an iota of confirmation.

To cite another example. A man sought advice from several friends; all gave him good advice, save one. He followed the advice of the one man. The results were predictably bad, and he was soon in a mess. Quite illogically, he blamed the man whose advice he had followed.

Now, two things were very clear. *First*, he had done what he had planned to do from the beginning. Some of his friends tried to talk to him out of it, but he persisted until he found one friend who agreed with him. *Second*, he had obviously wanted someone to agree with him, to give him the advice he wanted, in order to have someone to blame. In other words, people usually follow the advice they *want*, not the advice they *need*.

We do this as individuals, and we do it as a nation. Politicians regularly tell us, "The people must be heard," but they follow after strange counsels.

Advice-seeking can be a threat to freedom if, in seeking advice, we merely want confirmation of our opinions and someone to use as a scapegoat if our way proves to be a disaster. Advice-seeking then ceases to be a search for wisdom and counsel, but rather is an attempt to line up someone to take the blame. It is an exercise in irresponsibility rather than a course of wisdom.

Free men want to grow in understanding and take responsibility for their actions. Just a week ago, a broker friend told me of a bad experience with a client. He had called to ask that certain stocks be sold immediately, as soon as he hung up. The broker strongly advised against this, stating that the stock would soon rise sharply because of certain developments. The man refused; the holdings were sold at 9:30 A.M., and they rose dramatically at 1 P.M. and after. The man called back to blame his broker for selling as directed!

Long ago, Solomon told us that a fool loves his folly and goes back to it like a dog that returns to his vomit (Proverbs 26:11). Fools are the enemies of freedom because they love foolishness and reject wisdom.

★ *five* ★

WHAT IS HAPPENING TO PROSPERITY?

ALL OVER THE world, the post-World War II prosperity is steadily giving way to serious and deeply rooted economic problems. Not too many years ago, much was said about the economic miracles in West Germany. After World War II, Chancellor Erhard, influenced by the economist Roepke, led Germany back into a freer economy and into remarkable prosperity. Rising out of the ruins of the war, Germany soon became a very powerful economic force and a prosperous country.

Now, however, the German economy is in serious trouble, and its outlook is bleak and unpleasant. The reason for this amazing decline is readily apparent. The Germans have sought to outdo other European nations in their health, old-age, and welfare programs. As Alfred Zanker recently pointed out, "A wage earner gets six weeks' full pay while ill, then gets 80 percent of normal salary." (*U.S. News & World Report*, January 19, 1981, 32). German workers get a five-week paid vacation, and this may soon be extended to six weeks. Absenteeism is up to 8.4 percent of scheduled work time; it is 3.5 percent in the United States. Great numbers of foreign workers have come in to do work which Germans will not do. In fact, the foreign worker from the Mediterranean world is a growing factor in the populations of Germany, the Netherlands, Sweden, and other countries, just as illegal aliens are here in the United States.

As a result, West Germany is in trouble. Two key factors are evident in the German economic problem. *First*, welfarism has grown so rapidly that it has become an economic drag. Welfare, education, and the bureaucracy have grown to the point that they now command 47 percent of the national output.

Second, the work ethic is gone, or at best, declining. The mood is to relax and play, not to work and produce. Without a strong work ethic, no nation can long be strong.

Having said all this, we must then add that what is happening in West Germany is also happening in the United States, Sweden, Britain, and everywhere else. Statism and welfarism are growing, and morality and the work ethic are declining. All these things add up to economic woes.

To have a flourishing economy, we do need sound money and a healthy development in technology. Important as these things are, they are not enough. What is further needed is a sound moral foundation and a work ethic. Lacking these things, both an economy and a nation will decline, and freedom will also wane.

Throughout history, there has been a real connection between a work ethic, morality, and freedom. They go together. We live in a world of causality, not of happenstance. To be free, we must be responsible, godly, and productive. Like all things, freedom has a price.

★ *six* ★

WHY ARE JUDGES SUCH NITPICKERS?

WHY ARE TECHNICALITIES so heavily emphasized by our judges and courts, to the exclusion of justice? *New York* magazine (Jonathan Kirsch, "Is Anyone Safe Anymore," February 1981) described the accelerating crime rate and the declining convictions because of the emphasis on technicalities. Some frightening examples were cited. A Kern County, California, man was arrested for beating a coed to death. He waived his Miranda rights and talked to police. His conviction was reversed because, during the questioning, the man asked to see his mother. Because the police did not stop their examination to grant his request, the court held that his "rights" had been violated.

Another case: a young man confessed three times to murdering his parents and grandparents. The first confession was to a policeman, the second to a deputy district attorney, and the third to the television audience of *60 Minutes*. The conviction was reversed on the grounds that he did not understand his right to remain silent before he waived that right.

Many more cases can be cited. They are routine today. They should not surprise us, however.

After all, what is left to the law except technicalities if we deny justice? A prominent lawyer recently wrote a book ridiculing justice as a mythical idea. A major university professor and philosopher has also called the ideas of guilt and justice myths. Without agreeing with him, we can and must accept the fact that he has summed up the problem. According to the late Professor Walter Kaufmann, in *Without Guilt and Justice* (1973), there is no God; and therefore, there is neither guilt nor justice. For a man to be guilty requires that he be responsible to a higher being. For a law or justice to prevail over all men, there must again be a God over all. Having rejected God, Kaufmann logically rejected both guilt and justice. If we want justice, we must also accept God. Our problem today is that our federal and state governments and courts have rejected God. Therefore, they have rejected justice. All that is left of the law are empty technicalities.

Kaufmann held that "without justice there is no guilt." Our courts are turning loose the guilty because they no longer believe in justice. Having abandoned faith in God, they have abandoned justice. Justice is gone, and all that is left of the law are regulations which control the honest citizenry, strangle the businessman and farmer, and turn our country into a bureaucratic nightmare.

This should surprise no one. If God is meaningless to us, then justice and freedom will be meaningless also, and finally, life itself. The course we are on is suicidal. The wages of sin have always been death.

★ *seven* ★

IS THERE A DANGER IN BIBLICAL RELIGION?

ONE OF THE very strange facts of our time is that, as a part of our sex education classes in state schools, a variety of sexual practices, beginning with homosexuality, are given equal time with what Christendom has always regarded as normal sexuality. Some cities are going further. In one city, lesbians and homosexuals are brought in to defend their practices and to describe them. Students are asked to act out "gay" roles in class. According to one spokesman:

> We're not afraid to use graphic language to the kids, depending on the circumstances. We're the first group of out-front gays who've actually gone into schools — with sanction from the top. (*The Presbyterian Journal*, 4 February 1981, 11)

At the same time, of course, prayer has been banned from the schools, and the Bible also. Every year, we see protests and legal action at Christmas because some teacher uses Christmas carols or has a creche in the classroom.

It is not my concern here to argue on the pros and cons of prayer in the schools. I am simply calling attention to the gross inequity of barring religious practices common to most Americans while including in the classroom teaching the promotion of moral practices repugnant to most Americans.

Sexuality is more than a matter of technique, and no teaching in this area can be purely scientific. At every point, moral considerations enter in. Dr. Thomas Szarz, in *Sex By Prescription*, speaks of "this business of systematically concealing a secular sexual ethic as medical science and teaching it in the public schools as sex education" (117n). Dr. Szarz terms it, "religion as sex education."

Thus, we are indeed getting religion — humanistic religion — in the films, study materials, and teaching in the state schools. The U.S. Supreme Court has stated that humanism is a religion, so this status of humanism as a religion is a legal as well as historical fact. Why, then, should one religion command our state schools and others be banned? Why should humanistic teachings get tax support if we are, in principle, opposed (as I believe we should be), to the tax support of any religion?

Does the separation of church and state apply only to the Christian religion, but not to the religion of humanism?

This problem is of concern to millions of Americans. The domination of state schools and the financial assistance to one religion at the expense of others is offensive to many. The implicit position today seems to be that Biblical religion is a threat to our state schools, but that the religion of humanism is not. Such a position is provincial, unjust, and a threat to our freedom.

★ *eight* ★

ARE TAXES WIPING YOU OUT?

MORE THAN A few Americans are irritated and angry over the high cost of local, county, state, and federal government. Many of us who do not favor tax revolt can still understand the anger that leads men to refuse to pay taxes and so, in some cases, go to prison.

Consider the problem of a small landowner in Utah. Dean Frandsen leased out his property for oil production. His gross receipts in 1980 were $789 in royalties. Then the federal government collected a "windfall profits" tax. The result was that Frandsen's net income from his oil was $2.45. In disgust, he sent the remaining $2.45 to the federal government, stating, "The federal government may as well have it all" (*The Intellectual Activist*, vol. 1, October 1980, vol. 22).

In one area after another, taxes are becoming confiscatory. In 75 percent of all deaths, the family loses the house, farm, or business because of the inheritance tax. Very plainly, the federal government is in the business of robbing widows and orphans.

Very early in our history, a U.S. Supreme Court justice stated that the power to tax is the power to destroy. This is precisely what taxation has become in our day. It makes very little difference which party or administration is in power; the cost of civil government and our taxes go up and up. For most of us, our biggest — and also our greediest — dependent is the federal government.

In terms of this, it is interesting to reread the Declaration of Independence. What the colonists said in that document was that the British Crown, instead of being the defender of their liberties, had become their major enemy. In fact, the Declaration says that the Crown was engaged in a conspiracy to suppress and destroy American liberties. Bernard Bailyn, in *The Origin of American Politics*, stated that the leaders of the American colonies believed that there was a deliberate conspiracy on the part of the British Crown to reduce or to blot out their liberties. It was this conviction that led to the War for Independence. Men had come to distrust the normal political process and resorted to armed resistance.

Today, we have a similar cynicism about politics. Rightly or wrongly, millions of Americans believe that the modern state is interested in its own power, not in the people. People on the right and left are at odds on many things, but they are agreed in seeing the federal and state governments as a kind of conspiracy against the people. High taxes and pork-barrel federal policies tend to confirm this popular opinion.

If the federal and state governments want to restore any degree of stability to the national scene, they must stop this tax spiral and the resulting destruction of the people.

★ *nine* ★

IS OUR JUDICIAL SYSTEM BREAKING DOWN?

AN INCREASINGLY COMMON problem today is the decay and delay in our judicial system. In many cases where a criminal is caught in the act, a dismissal results after many delays and postponements of the trial. The reason is that, after a period of time, witnesses move away or die and the charges are dismissed.

In civil suits, the matter is even worse. In some of our major cities, it takes almost five years for a civil case to come to trial. The practical consequences of this are far-reaching. Where money and property are tied up, how many people can afford to wait five years?

One retired judge in Los Angeles has said recently that the costs of civil suits are so great that it does not pay to sue unless more than $20,000 is at stake. This means that, for most of us, the courts offer no hope in civil cases. In criminal cases, a crime committed against us or our property will cost us far more than it will the offender.

Very plainly, our legal system is failing to fulfill its purpose. Instead of providing us with courts of justice, it is providing us with roadblocks to justice. One criminal lawyer, in answer to complaints about continual postponements and delaying tactics, said, "If all we wanted from the system was instant justice, we could all look to Ayatollah Khalkhali or Idi Amin."

Are these the alternatives: the tyranny of arbitrary courts on the one hand, or the tyranny of courts which never function on the other? Is there not an alternative of justice fairly and quickly administered?

One of our problems is that the courts themselves have created so many roadblocks and technical exceptions to judicial process that the passage of justice has become an unduly slow and constipated process. In some instances, as much time is spent now in selecting a jury as was once spent on an entire case. Appellate courts reverse decisions on trifling details, and retrials become necessary. The arbitrary reversals by the U.S Supreme Court result in paralysis in the lower courts, as judges lean backwards to avoid endangering a case by giving the Supreme Court any grounds to overrule them.

The Sixth Amendment to the Constitution guarantees to the accused in all criminal prosecutions "the right to a speedy and public trial." Today, many of the accused do *not* want a speedy trial; they gain more by many long delays. What we need is some kind of guarantee to victims, and to the public, of a speedy trial of all those accused of some kind of crime. The guarantee should work both ways, or else the innocent, and freedom itself, will be penalized.

★ *ten* ★

WHAT HAS HAPPENED TO INTEGRITY?

IN RECENT YEARS, we have had a series of reports on very extensive frauds in the scientific world. Several years ago, *Science Digest* gave a detailed report on the high degree of dishonesty in reporting research; fraudulent claims are made by scientists, and when these claims are shown to be false, usually nothing is done to punish the offender.

More recently, *U.S. News & World Report* (March 2, 1981) reported on scandals in medical institutions across the country. Specific cases were cited: fabricated data on anorexia nervosa, on cancer therapy, on Hodgkin's Disease, on skin grafts, and more. One case was described as "the Watergate of science," an all too mild a description. Watergate represented one act; these scientific frauds represent a whole chain of operation.

The implications of such frauds are deadly. A variety of medical, psychological, and educational practices ensue from such research. These practices assume a foundation of scientific data to be true when it is, in reality, false. These false data affect your life and mine, as well as the practices of those who assume their truth and work with patients on that basis. Such fraud is criminal in its meaning, and yet only rarely is there even a dismissal of such scientists. Only after some flagrant cases did the National Institutes of Health establish a "debarment" procedure to end all further federal grants of funds to researchers found guilty of fraud.

Revolting as all this is, we should not be surprised. We are getting what we asked for. We have separated the need and requirement of a godly character from the acquisition of knowledge. Should we be surprised if men of learning and science prove, then, to be only members of a scientific mafia? A doctor or a scientist (as well an educator) with a great deal of learning, but no character, is only a more dangerous man—not a better one. Education makes a man learned, not moral. Just because a man has several degrees, a prestigious position, and an important status, no more makes him a good man than a million dollar house in the best neighborhood makes a member of a criminal syndicate a good citizen.

As a people, we have poured billions into teaching facts to youth, but almost nothing into making them aware of the meaning of godly faith and character. As a result, in every area of life, we see a lack of integrity, honesty, and morality.

For freedom to survive requires more than a literate people; it necessitates a public character marked by a godly faith, integrity, and morality. These things are inseparable from freedom.

★ *eleven* ★

WHAT HAS HAPPENED TO THE MIDDLE CLASS?

HISTORICALLY, THE UNITED States has been the great country of the middle class. The extremes of wealth and poverty have been less prevalent here, and the great majority of Americans were in the middle class, neither rich nor poor, but stable, responsible, and public-spirited.

These middle-class families have been the mainstay of churches, charitable causes, political action, and social responsibilities. It has been their social and religious concerns which have been largely responsible for what America is.

Today, that picture is changing because of inflation. The middle class is being wiped out step by step. To make ends meet and avoid falling below the poverty line, or coming close to it, in millions of marriages it is necessary for both husband and wife to work. Most of this is not career work on the part of women, but necessary work to survive. It creates problems. As one young woman said, "We cannot afford either a house or a child unless I work, and if I work, keeping house and having a baby becomes more difficult."

With the present cost of housing and the high rate of interest, even with both husband and wife working, a house is beyond their reach. In many areas across the United States, the monthly payments on even a modest house are prohibitive.

Inflation is the guilty party in this situation. Inflation is a product of federal spending and the federally controlled increase of the money supply. During the years 1976 to 1980, the money supply increased by over $220 billion, more than one-fourth of the total since 1933. Inflation has thus begun to gallop. The result is that all of us have been hurt. Our real income is less, and we are less and less able to make ends meet.

We have been a middle-class country, but the middle class is now close to disaster. In almost every case where a people have been taken over by a tyrant state, by a dictatorship, or by a fascist or socialist regime, a severe inflation preceded the death of freedom. Inflation is the destruction of both economic and political freedom, and inflation is our problem today. Unless we control and eliminate inflation, we ourselves will be a controlled people, and freedom will be eliminated. The inflation rate can be compared to a barometer: as the inflation rate goes up, freedom diminishes and begins to die.

★ SERIES SIX ★

★ *one* ★

WHO GETS THE BENEFITS FROM WELFARISM?

POVERTY PROGRAMS, AS operated by federal, state, and local governmental agencies, are an expensive item for every taxpayer. The total cost, as of 1980, was $200 billion every year. This is an indication of perhaps some kind of concern for the poor, but is it any solution to the problems of poverty? A Temple University professor (according to *Review of the News*, March 3, 1981) pointed out: "If we simply gave the money to the poor, each eligible family of four would get close to $40,000 a year."

The poor, however, get no such income from our welfare agencies. In fact, their income from welfare in no way resembles the appropriations for welfare. According to a Hoover Institute economist: "The poor are a gold mine. By the time they are studied, advised, experimented with, and administered, the poor have helped many a middle-class liberal to achieve affluence with government money."

Obviously, some money must be spent to administer welfare. The problem is that these federal, state, and local bureaucracies are spending a disproportionate amount for administration, to the point where welfare programs are better for the welfare of the bureaucracies than for the poor. We should not be surprised that welfare has become a growth industry. Welfarism does more for the state, its power, and its bureaucracy than it does for the poor.

Some cities and many states have very strict rules controlling every private or religious charity. No solicitation of funds is permitted unless very strict rules are complied with, and in some instances, groups not meeting the rules are put on a blacklist. Some of these rules are common sense requirements to prevent fraud; others tend to be unreasonable. The important fact is that various state agencies would not qualify if a like set of rules applied to them. There are abuses in the private sector, but these are few and exceptional, whereas the abuses on the part of statist agencies are commonplace and flagrant.

More than a few writers of recent years, including George Gilder, have shown that welfarism is a detriment to the poor and a breeding ground for a large variety of social problems. To this we can add that it is now becoming apparent that the major beneficiary of welfarism has been a power-hungry state. In other words, it is the federal, state, and local agencies of civil government that get the real benefits from welfarism. The poor (and the taxpayers) are the victims of it.

In the name of welfare, we have been creating a power state.

★ *two* ★

IS DEATH BY "GOVERNMENT" PERMISSION ONLY?

RECENTLY, THE NEWSLETTER *The Intellectual Activist* spoke of the possibility of death by government permission only. What this periodical referred to was that twelve states are considering legislation to restrict the freedom of businesses to close down. Before long, if such legislation is enacted, being broke or without customers will be no excuse. The details vary from state to state, but the proposals seek to protect the jobs of all employees.

Such legislation raises some interesting questions. Why not make it illegal for tenants to move out and leave an apartment owner with empty units? Again, why not make it illegal for a car to need repairs for four years or tires to wear out before so many miles of usage? If we can abolish by law the right to go broke, why not abolish the right to die? Can we extend man's life expectancy by making it illegal to die before the age of a hundred without a heavy fine?

How about some legislation against drought and floods, or against scorching heat? I am almost afraid to suggest such nonsense, for fear someone will take me seriously! Legislators I know tell me of the sometimes far-out measures which are put into the hopper.

In 1971, I was in the San Fernando Valley of California when a disastrous earthquake hit on February 9 at about 6 A.M.. For a few days, there were aftershocks, which left people a bit nervous. Everywhere, people spoke about the earthquake. The classic line came from a woman in a supermarket checkout line, whom I heard say, "Why doesn't the government do something about it?"

Our problem today is that the "government" is doing something about almost everything, and doing it badly. We are treated as incompetents by federal officials, as though we are stupid children in need of being controlled. Recently, a very able businessman went to an Internal Revenue Service office for an audit. After about two hours of treatment as a bad boy and an incompetent, he asked for a restroom break. He told me he was almost tempted to raise one or two fingers and ask, "Please, teacher, can I go?"

Any time we are treated as anything less than responsible adults, our freedom is threatened. Children do need supervision, care, and a certain amount of control, but adults need freedom to exercise their maturity. The whole foundation of Christianity and our form of civil government presupposes our responsibility and freedom. Moral choices are free choices. Freedom and responsibility are inseparable. The less freedom in a society, the less the responsibility.

★ *three* ★

ARE SPORTS BECOMING A THREAT TO US?

I HAVE ALWAYS enjoyed sports, and I can remember my excitement as a boy in watching my first big-league game. As Americans, we are prone to delight in sports, but not to the extremes of some countries. For us, a game is a game — fun, but not much more than that.

Recently, however, there have been developments on the sport scene which may in time create an ugly backlash against these really good games. For some years, some baseball, football, basketball, and hockey teams have been provided with publicly owned facilities built specifically for them at the taxpayer's expense. Of the eighty stadiums and arenas housing the nearly a hundred big-league teams, according to *Inquiry* magazine (May 1981), about two-thirds were built at the taxpayer's expense.

These stadiums and arenas are not only a tremendous expense to the taxpayer, but are often scandal-tainted in their construction. Their costs are astronomical, some are badly located and poorly constructed, and the main beneficiaries are the owners of the sports teams. These owners are already extremely wealthy, but we pay for their benefit a considerable amount of taxes.

If sports are entitled to public housing at the taxpayer's expense, why not other activities? Why not provide free barbershops for all barbers — plush facilities for a modest rental fee? After all, virtually all males use barbershops, so they serve more people than do the big league sports!

About 50 to 60 percent of all Americans go to church. Should we build churches with tax funds? Restaurants provide a very much needed public service, and their costs are high and their life-expectancy not too good. Should we subsidize restaurant construction and maintenance?

Of course, the big league teams pay a rent for the use of the stadiums and arenas. This amount is small, usually 5 to 6 percent of the gate receipts, with the frequent condition that this payment is valid only after a minimum attendance figure is reached. Are you paying only 5 to 6 percent of your income for rent or house payments? Are you excused from payments if your income drops below a certain amount? Why, then, do we have to pay to provide housing for big league sports? I like sports, but not on my tax bill!

In brief, the kinds of things our taxes now subsidize are not only ridiculous, but dangerous to our freedom. When the modest-income taxpayer is subsidizing housing for wealthy big league teams, something is seriously wrong and needs altering.

★ *four* ★

ARE REGULATIONS COSTING TOO MUCH?

RECENTLY, A MAN who operates a business told me that a considerable part of his time is spent in filling out state and federal forms. "I'm a bookkeeper for the bureaucrats," he complained.

However, it is not only private citizens who make such complaints. Fred Heddinger, executive director of the Pennsylvania State School Board Association, has released an interesting bit of information. In 1979, the State of Pennsylvania got approximately 7.5 cents of its educational dollar from the federal government, but it cost the state 8 cents of that dollar to comply with the federal regulations and administer the funds (*Capsule*, November 1980, 14).

Now, such an expense could be justified *if* education were improved by federal regulations. After all, it is unwise to reduce education to a matter of cost only. The results determine the value of the expenditures.

However, the quality of education has declined as federal controls have increased. The experts in Washington feel that they have more knowledge and ability to provide quality education than the local school board. Congress and the bureaucracy have seized more and more control over education, supposedly to improve educational quality and opportunity. The result has instead been a steady decline in quality and in opportunity. The result has been a backlash taking three forms: *first*, demand for more local control over state schools; *second*, the growth and development of Christian schools all over the country; *third*, the development of various plans for home teaching.

The unhappy fact is that Washington is not getting the message that regulations are costing too much in money, in manpower and wasted time, and in the destruction of quality. Moreover, what has happened in education has taken place elsewhere as well. Regulations are stifling the economy, personal freedoms, and the quality of life generally.

Like narcotics addicts, our society is becoming hooked on federal funds. Sports, arts and sciences, education, big business, and more all look to Washington for handouts. The last thing many seem to want is *freedom*. An editorial in the *Capsule* sums it up:

> A society that is hooked on federal funds is one that has totally detached itself from the ideologies of Christianity and has swallowed the humanistic "funding fable" hook, line, and sinker. (*Capsule*, November 1980, 9)

It is time for us to unhook ourselves.

★ *five* ★

WHAT IS A FUMAGE?

THE WORD "FUMAGE" is something you find only in an unabridged dictionary, but it deals with something very much a part of our world today: *taxation*. Tyrant states tax everything they can think of, and a new way of stripping people of their money is a delight to them. The old Turkish Empire, among other things, taxed trees. Shade trees were cut down, and the hills stripped of trees, to avoid extra taxation. The sultans also had a window tax. Houses were, as a result, built virtually windowless.

A fumage was a tax from Anglo-Saxon England — a hearth tax, or literally, a tax on smoke. I am rather afraid to talk about the fumage, lest some state legislators get ideas about another source of taxation. Every fireplace and cooking hearth, however primitive, was taxed by the king.

Taxation is a very interesting (as well as ugly) fact. Every country in history has moved, step by step, towards increasing taxes, until finally the burden of taxation grows so great that the people rebel, the civil government collapses, and a new civil order is begun. Then the same old process begins, sometimes very early. The French Revolution protested against the king's taxes and rule, only to increase the taxes upon gaining power and to overrule in new and unprecedented ways.

Has any country reversed the destructive course of taxation without bloodshed? Here the record is very bleak indeed. Taxation has always been like a cancer. It grows and spreads until it destroys the entire body politic.

Is there, then, no hope? Are we doomed to seeing taxation increase until we are economically destroyed and the nation collapses? Well, one ray of hope has appeared. A few years ago, California passed a proposition which rivaled and surpasses Lexington, Concord, and the shot heard round the world. Property taxes were drastically cut by a popular ballot initiative measure. This measure caught on in various states. But it was not enough, and the impetus is now faltering and waning.

The choice is a clear one. Increasing the tax burden leads to economic decay and social revolution. Cutting taxes dramatically and ruthlessly can lead to a rebirth of freedom. Taxation—like cancer—can sometimes require drastic surgery. Are we ready for it?

★ *six* ★

WHO IS PROTECTING US?

IN AN ARTICLE in *New York* magazine (May 25, 1981), Edward N. Costikyan and Maxwell Lehman called attention to an ugly fact:

> It has become a platitude, bitterly true, that people are afraid, that the streets have been taken over by muggers. The police can't protect the residents, although that duty is the first obligation of government. ("How Neighborhoods Could Help Themselves," 8)

This is a grim and ugly fact. If two men who are involved in politics tell us that our civil government is no longer able to meet its first obligation — to protect the people — then we are really in trouble. There is no question that civil government today is trying to do everything under the sun, and doing nothing at all successfully. In terms of efficiency and effectiveness, the only thing that civil government does at all well is to take money away from us.

Having said this, we must add that the fault is by no means entirely on the side of civil authorities. Lawlessness is so widespread and extensive that it is becoming impossible to control. I can still recall the whining of one man at a neighborhood meeting about how the police were not doing their job. The fact was that his boys were the neighborhood menace. We have no right to complain about the failures of the police if we are creating a part of their problem by failing to train our children properly.

The church has always been the main force for law enforcement. By the religious and moral instruction it gives, the church has been America's greatest law enforcement agency. This, however, is not true now of many churches. Neither sound doctrine nor sound morals seem to be present in many Sunday-school lessons and pulpit expositions. To teach Sunday-school children about American Indian cultures and aspirations and nothing about the Ten Commandments is hardly sound teaching of morality. Instead of being a moral force in the community, such churches become a disintegrating force, and the children are robbed of the moral discipline and faith they so greatly need.

Moreover, government (like charity) begins at home. The failure of the family to discipline its children is a key contributing factor to our moral decline.

Today, government is indeed failing to protect its citizens, but the failure begins at more basic levels than the police. It represents the moral failure of the churches, families, and individuals of our country. Whatever else an election might do, and whoever we may vote in, we cannot alter or erase the moral failure. It begins where we live. The remedy also begins there.

★ *seven* ★

HAVE WE LOST OUR MANNERS?

HAVE WE LOST our manners? Very obviously, people are not as mannerly now as they once were. My favorite story on old-fashioned courtliness and humor goes back to the days of Theodore Roosevelt's presidency. In those days, Washington was a small city, and the area had few people. Roosevelt loved to take friends on hikes around the Potomac River and the marsh area. On one hike on a hot day, when the group halted, Roosevelt suggested that they take a swim. All the men stripped and dove into the river, swimming in the nude. Roosevelt noticed, however, that the French ambassador, Jean Jules Jusserand, had removed everything except his gloves. "Mr. Ambassador," asked the nude Roosevelt, "have you not forgotten your gloves?" The debonair Frenchman replied, "We might meet ladies."

There is something to be said for an era with that kind of wit and presence of mind.

Manners can become absurd and can be overly stressed, but they do serve to keep people from manifesting their uglier feelings and dispositions, and civilization needs that restraint.

Too often, for example, our news commentators, cartoonists, and politicians are unmannerly to the extreme. Anyone who disagrees with them is a menace to civilization, a fascist beast, the enemy of the people, and so on. We are seeing increasingly the disappearance of all manners towards people who disagree with us. Civilized discourse requires and depends on treating those who disagree with us as entitled to courtesy, respect, and a fair-minded attention.

To break the rules of mannerly discourse is a prelude to social violence and civil disorders. It means that we regard the other person as mentally hopeless and therefore only amenable to coercion and violence.

Manners are important because they presuppose that the best way to change the other person is to show respect, concern, and courtesy towards him. We cannot convert someone by first spitting in his face! When we deny that people can be changed, reached, or approached by means of good manners, we are also saying that freedom is a useless thing and that coercion and violence alone will "persuade" people.

Respect and courtesy for those with whom we disagree is a necessary prerequisite for a free society. The intemperance, venom, and sometimes studied insolence of much of our public discourse is a threat to freedom.

★ *eight* ★

IS IT SAFE TO RELY ON THE LAW?

IN THIS AGE of overprotection, we have laws and regulations to protect us from every kind of problem and from fraud. How good are these laws and codes?

Someone I know had a house built, a very superior one in design and planning. He moved into it happily, only to encounter some problems, some minor and some not so minor. One serious problem was the fireplace, which began to leave the house. Now, the house had been built according to code, had been inspected, and met all specifications. In such a situation, what do you do? The building department of the county said it was a matter between himself and the masonry firm. The mason had gone out of business under another name, so the original contracting firm was now nonexistent. As a result, my friend had to pay for the redoing of a job built according to code (supposedly) and approved. The building code gave him no protection when he needed it.

Another friend moved into a newly-built house, and after the first heavy storm, the builder was back to crawl through the attic to check on the roof, to examine things under the house, and then to make a minor change or two to insure doubly that no problem would ensue. My friend was protected not by the code, but by the contractor.

The difference in the two cases was character. The building code was in both cases the same. No building code, however good, can replace character. In our day, we rely too much on laws and building codes to protect us, and too little on character. As a result, we are more easily exploited by unscrupulous men. No code can be framed which a crooked man will not twist, exploit, or corrupt. By placing our confidence in laws and codes, we are asking for trouble. We are forgetting, too, that the soundest basis for a sound economy and a trustworthy job is character.

I passed a proposed subdivision recently. The builder behind it has left dissatisfaction everywhere, as well as threats of lawsuits. When ready, this subdivision will likely draw eager buyers because their presumption will be that the strict building codes will protect them. The net result is that the most important single consideration of all is overlooked — the character of the builder. After all, who nowadays doubts the character of a successful man whose sales offices are plush and beguiling places? Who needs character references when he smells of success?

★ *nine* ★

IS A THING GOOD BECAUSE IT'S NEW?

A FEW YEARS ago, someone observed, "In Europe they say 'It's good because it's old.'" To a great degree, this is true. In fashions, the key is not what is most becoming to us, but what is new and current in the world of styles. We waddle around in baggy pants or skin-tight pants, in long dresses or mini-skirts, depending on what is new and therefore stylish. In fact, we have equated the stylish with the new and the faddish, not with good taste.

The basic motivation in being current with the world of styles is a follow the sheep mentality. For all too many people, it does not matter how monstrous they look, provided it is the latest look and one that draws attention.

In all of this, what we have forgotten is that when a people are so sensitive to current fads, they are also mindless and prone to be a mob. To be so concerned with being current with the styles and fads of the world is to be not only mindless, but also very susceptible to totalitarianism.

One of the ugliest facts about adolescence in our day is that the teenager sees it as almost a matter of life and death to do what everyone else is doing. To be different from the crowd is traumatic to the teenager. It is difficult to imagine a worse preparation for adulthood and maturity than such a perspective.

Lately, of course, we have had a craving for something besides the new in some areas. Nostalgia has led to a desire for collectibles and antiques. Antiques, however, like new things, are not necessarily better — nor necessarily worse. Neither being old nor being new makes a thing necessarily good. In fact, nothing would be a more heartening sign of maturity than an emphasis on what is *good* rather than old or new. Quality, not age nor youth, counts, and quality should be our concern in people and things.

I find it distressing to hear people hark back to the past, as though only then were things good. "The good old days" were often far from good. It is equally unpleasant to hear others talk as though everything good came into the world only yesterday or this morning. It is not time, age, or youth that gives quality to anything or anyone, but character itself. Long ago, the prophet Zephaniah said, "[S]eek righteousness" (or justice) (Zeph. 2:3), and Solomon declared, "The heart of him that hath understanding seeketh knowledge" (Prov. 15:14). Their words stand forever true.

★ *ten* ★

ARE WE APPROPRIATING FUNDS FOR NONSENSE?

U.S. SENATOR PROXMIRE once called attention to various absurdities for which federal funds are regularly appropriated. "Tip" O'Neill, Speaker of the House, reported on some of the strange things written into the budget. O'Neill said, "Once a doctor came down here to talk to us. He said the average dwarf grows only forty-six inches high, and if we appropriated $45 million for research, maybe that could be increased to fifty-two inches. So I got the $45 million into the budget."

Now, perhaps if you and I were dwarfs, we might want to be six inches taller, but would we be justified in asking Congress for funds to study the problem? Millions of American men are going bald; is it the duty of Congress to appropriate funds for hair-growing research? Some women are very upset about being flat-chested. Should we appropriate millions of dollars to research the subject? Wouldn't it be cheaper to suggest that they look for men who prefer flat-chested women, as some do?

In other words, why tax our fellow citizens for our problems? Why make purely personal concerns the subject of national legislation and taxation?

Of course, many of these appropriations are sought by the scientific establishment as means of providing them with research funds and facilities. It was, after all, not the dwarfs but a doctor who approached O'Neill for funding research on the matter. Most likely, the major beneficiary of the research will be the scientific establishment, as is usually the case.

Not surprisingly, there is a growing distrust of the scientific establishment because of its plundering of the public treasury for a vast variety of sometime trifling causes. Of course, funding scientific research is part of our national elitism. Together with this funding of research, we have the funding of the arts because we have decided that "culture" (defined as the arts) is important. Why not fund baseball and make millions of Americans happy, or football and sports on television? Films and television are important aspects of popular "culture." Why not fund them through congressional appropriations?

Or, better, why not stop funding all of them and let "the private sector" fund whatever it wishes to see prosper? Why should we not have a freedom from conscripted and compulsory support for causes of no concern to us or which are hostile to our own interests and ideas? Why not try freedom?

★ *eleven* ★

ARE WE ENEMIES OF INITIATIVE?

EVERY NOW AND then, a brief news item catches my eye, then nothing more appears and I am left wondering how the incident turned out. One such item appeared in November 1976:

> The Ohio Division of Wildlife recently used as many as five agents, including two undercover men, to investigate and prosecute an 11-year-old boy for selling fishing worms and crayfish in his parents' front yard. In two weeks his stand sold $4.50 worth of bait, including that sold to the undercover agents. State regulations in Ohio require a permit to sell bait. (*Libertarian Party News*, November–December 1976, cited in Leslie Snyder's *Justice or Revolution*, 113)

This is not an unusual story; I have run across several like it. I keep wondering, however, what happened. How could grown men make such an arrest without being somewhat embarrassed? Were they not ashamed to be involved in such a case? Did the state of Ohio do anything to alter its laws? Talk about juvenile delinquency! Legislators who pass such a law, and bureaucrats and agents who enforce it, are worse than delinquent.

Long ago, the psalmist spoke of the throne of iniquity framing "mischief by a law" (Ps. 94:20); that is, using the pretense of law to be oppressive. I submit that our lawmakers today are framing mischief by law.

At the same time that children are arrested for showing initiative and a desire to earn some money, our wise fathers in the state capitols and Washington, D.C., are whittling away at parental powers and the freedom of children, and our courts are taking over parental powers.

Let's get back to the boy in Ohio. When civil government uses five agents to entrap an eleven-year-old boy for selling fishing worms, something is radically wrong with the country. If they are ready to go after an eleven-year-old with such passion, what will they not do to us when they so chose?

I said that I have often wondered how that story, and others like it, ended. However, in a very important sense, the story will not end until we do something about it. This means, at the very least, clipping the wings of the power state. It means valuing freedom more highly than statist regulations. Moreover, it means regarding all state and federal officials who are involved in such cases as the moral lepers that they are.

What was wrong with selling fishing worms? Is it possible to sell inferior or defective fishing worms? Why is a permit necessary to sell bait? Is the state trying to prove to us that we have no freedom to do anything unless they give us a permit?

★ *twelve* ★

DO TAXPAYERS HAVE ANY RIGHTS?

IN 1979, LESLIE Snyder, in her book, *Justice or Revolution*, called attention to the fact that taxpayers have fewer rights than accused murderers. The accused murderer has the following rights:

> He is innocent until proven guilty
>
> Is informed of his constitutional rights
>
> Need not give evidence against himself
>
> Is entitled to trial by jury
>
> Prosecutor may not also be the judge
>
> May not be prosecuted on basis of illegally obtained evidence
>
> May not be punished on testimony of secret informers who cannot be cross examined
>
> May not be subjected to fines and punishments without due process of law. (148)

The taxpayer has none of these rights. In other words, our laws regard the taxpayer as a dangerous man entitled to none of the "rights" granted to accused murderers.

Now, I am not in favor of the tax revolt, but I can most certainly understand why it is spreading. When a country places penalties on its taxpayers which are not imposed upon suspected criminals, a number of people will most certainly rebel against the situation.

Moreover, it creates a very dangerous climate of opinion. As I travel back and forth across the country, I find that a very large (and growing) number of people believe that the police spend more time writing out traffic tickets than trying to solve crimes. The traffic ticket is another tax on the tax-paying citizenry, who resent the failure to solve most crimes and the readiness to tax or ticket the people. More than once, I have been told that city councils stress traffic tickets as a means of additional revenues.

The American people resent injustice, and they are naturally rebellious. They do not take kindly to being exploited—and they do feel exploited. Taxation has become a means of exploitation.

At the same time, it is an unhealthy situation whenever and wherever the people begin to regard their own civil government as the enemy. It means that the civil government has become hostile to freedom and is at war with its own people. In such a setting, lawlessness proliferates and anarchy begins to take over.

The purpose of civil government should be the protection of the people, not their exploitation by taxation. Do you feel protected, or exploited and overtaxed? A growing number of Americans feel exploited and overtaxed.

★ *thirteen* ★

WHAT IS LEGAL TENDER?

THE TERM *"legal tender"* refers to money. It defines lawful money which is valid for all debts public and private. Our paper money carries the term *legal tender* on its face, yet the term was once denounced by great Americans as a fraud.

The Reverend John Witherspoon, one of the signers of the Declaration of Independence, declared that legal tender was a way of requiring by law that bad money (or bad checks or paper money) be accepted as valid. If money is good money, no law is needed to make men accept it. If the money is bad or depreciating, men will try to hold their assets in other ways.

Another great American, Noah Webster, attacked the legal tender doctrine in 1790 with these words:

> A (legal) tender law is the devil. When I trust a man a sum of money, I expect he will return the full value. That legislature which says my debtor may pay me with one-third of the value he received commits a deliberate act of villainy; an act for which an individual, in any government, would be honored with a whipping-post, and in most governments, with a gallows . . .
>
> But legislatures can, with the solemn face of rulers and guardians of justice, boldly give currency to an adulterated coin, enjoin it upon debtors to cheat their creditors, and enforce their systematic knavery with legal penalties. The difference between the man who makes and passes counterfeit money, and the man who renders his creditor one-third of the value

> of the debt and demands a discharge, is the same as between a thief and a robber.
>
> My countrymen, the devil is among you. (Leslie Snyder, *Justice or Revolution*, 125)

Many other great Americans held this view; for example, Patrick Henry. Daniel Webster held that the idea of legal tender is alien to the Constitution, which defines money as gold and silver.

Now, what was once the constitutional and moral view of money is no longer heard in high places. Our view of money has changed because our perspective is statist, not moral. This idea that money is good because the federal government tells us it is, is the legal-tender concept.

The Founding Fathers, however, held a contrary view: money, they believed, is good only if it is good money—gold or silver—with a recognized value. For them, a state-ordained legal tender was bad money, and the worst kind of bad money. We have come a long way from their opinion. The difference spells a loss of freedom.

★ SERIES SEVEN ★

★ *one* ★

IS HAPPINESS A CRIME?

SEVERAL TIMES, I have seen a news item in several magazines with very different political principles. This news item was a startling one, but it rang true to so much in our world today. In Lancashire, England, Harry and Esther Hough have been foster parents to over 140 children in four years. They decided to adopt some children, but the local social services agencies denied their application, saying, "Both of you have had few, if any, negative experiences when children yourselves, and also seem to enjoy a marital experience where rows and arguments have no place." The letter went on to say that adoption could not be approved because the children would have insufficient exposure to negative experiences (*The Intellectual Activist*, August 15, 1981, 4).

In other words, a happy marriage and home were said to be a liability! Happiness was treated as though it would endanger the mental outlook of the adopted children!

I thought again of the Houghs and their predicament when a friend described a guided trip into the mountains. The young guide spoiled the entire trip by insisting on his right to lecture against pollution. The entire area was national forest; there was no threat of any exploitation of the area, but the guide's perspective was that for people to relax and enjoy the wilderness trip was somehow immoral unless they paid the price of some miserable lectures.

We live in an age of killjoys who are determined to make us miserable over something. Their attitude is that, in a world full of problems, how dare we be happy? Such ranters want to make people feel miserable if they enjoy a good meal and then relax before the television set to watch a favorite program. They do not want us to have any freedom from problems. If we are not bemoaning or demonstrating over something, we are somehow moral wretches because we sometimes sit down and relax or because we are really happy and enjoy life.

I believe these killjoys are a threat to freedom, as well to the solution of problems. Because they exaggerate every problem, they make people skeptical of everything they say. Lacking balance, they turn people off. Moreover, their totalitarian mentality is very real; unless you are as intense and miserable as they are over every problem, you are (in their eyes) a moral reprobate. In fact, happiness is as real in this world as are problems. We dare not deny the reality of either, nor turn our backs on happiness or problems. The Bible tells us in 1 Peter 3:7 that life itself is a grace and to be enjoyed as such. Those who deny the grace of life, and its joys, will soon lose their freedom also.

★ *two* ★

WHY IS CRIME A GROWTH INDUSTRY?

IN A WORLD where the city streets are becoming dangerous, and a house is no security, freedom becomes very limited. According to *New York* magazine (*New York*, September 14, 1981, 35f.), New York City has around 13,000 convicted killers on the streets; some of these have served up to thirty years in prison, others only a few months' probation. The article, by Michael Daley, was titled "Double Jeopardy," and all of us are in multiple jeopardy today because of crime. Daly cites cases such as one of a murderer released as fairly well prepared to rejoin his community after serving two months who, two months and twenty-seven days after his release, killed another man.

Across the country, such horror stories can be repeated over and over again. We can recognize that some serious problems in law enforcement exist, and that our courts are part of the problem. Having said this, we must look elsewhere for the problem. In the 1940s, despite a depression, the streets of New York and other places were clearly safer. Many smaller communities had very few policemen, and these officers had very little to do. Why is the United States so much more crime prone today? Why is it that even the public schools are a high crime area?

I believe that some of the blame must be laid at the doors of the public schools, with their humanistic value system and their inadequate ability to educate. Most of the responsibility, however, belongs to neither the courts nor the public schools (bad as they are) but to the churches. They are no longer providing the solidly Biblical teaching and training which is their responsibility. As far as some churches are concerned, these are the last places to go to find some honestly Biblical faith.

George Washington, in his farewell address, warned us all against expecting any public morality without the foundation of a solidly religious training and education. It was, he held, not possible to have the one without the other. Public life is a reflection of religious faith.

Our public life today is the reflection of a hedonistic humanism, of a belief that it is a dog-eat-dog world, and that every man should claw and grab to get what he wants. Our police did not make these problems, and our courts, however incompetent, did not create the lawless populace. Countless churches, by their moral and religious waywardness and delinquency, have helped create a lawless generation. Now that our streets and homes grow less and less safe, freedom from God, sexual freedom, and freedom from disciplines of learning and life seem less and less like freedom and more and more like the prelude to a new slavery. We may still have the freedom to vote, but how much is that freedom worth if the walk to the polling booth is not safe for many elderly citizens?

★ *three* ★

ARE YOU AFRAID OF THE TAXMAN?

I HEARD A Western rancher, a fine and able man, admit to fear: he is afraid of the IRS taxmen. They have all the resources of the federal government behind them, and a lone man can rarely afford to fight them.

I thought of his comment as I read a news report that there are about 71,000 federal, state, and local agencies in the United States with the power to levy taxes, direct or indirect (*Inquiry*, September 1, 1981, 2). My friend was worried about one big bad wolf at the door; we have an army of them!

It seems ironic to think that the United States began with a tax-protest movement over a very minor tax as compared to today. We now pay a higher percentage of our income in taxes in a day than the colonists paid in a year. Granted, there were other very important political considerations in 1776, but we have all those problems with us now, only greatly magnified.

Did you know that you have no absolute legal right to any of your income? The Sixteenth Amendment — the income tax amendment — has not a single restricting clause. Congress is given a blank check with respect to our income. This is why what we are allowed to keep is called an exemption. It takes an act of Congress to tell us what we can keep for ourselves.

If this sounds grim, it is simply because it is so. With all the talk about the power of private lobbies representing capital, labor, education, the taxpayers, and so on, why don't we hear about the 71,000 governmental agencies with powers to tax us? Does anyone imagine that this vast bureaucratic empire ever works for lower taxes?

All too often when we hear screams from Washington about funds to the needy and aged being cut, what the screamers really mean is that funds to an imperial bureaucracy are being cut.

It is interesting to note that when the tsar was overthrown in Old Russia, and the Bolsheviks took over, the same old bureaucracy went marching on, growing bigger and steadily more powerful than ever before. Civil governments, in this age of revolutions, come and go, but the bureaucracies stay and keep on growing. Few people get worked up over them, but their empires expand steadily.

We all make noises about the defects of one president after another, usually with good reason, but we forget that the presidents accomplish little as compared with the vast bureaucracies and the 71,000 taxing bodies. These are the agencies which are steadily and quietly eating our freedom.

Seventy-one thousand taxing agencies in the United States, and God only knows how many thousands of bureaucrats in all these agencies! No wonder our freedom is waning!

★ *four* ★

ARE YOU FILTHY RICH ON $10,000 A YEAR?

I CAN RECALL, not too many years after World War II, hearing someone who made $10,000 a year labeled as "filthy rich." In fact, I once saw an old movie (one of the earliest Cary Grant pictures, I think) in which some women described the hero as very rich because he has an income of $5,000 a year! Of course, one of my university professors described how rich he felt with his big job, at $20 a month in gold.

Well, inflation has changed things since then. Everybody knows that, except the taxman. Nowadays, $10,000 a year puts one far below the poverty line; no one is "filthy rich" on that amount! What $5,000 would buy in 1940, $15,000 would not buy in 1970, and certainly not in 1980 or 1981. Inflation has gone from 1 or 2 percent to 10 and 15 percent, and everyone's real income has decreased. Very few of us get pay raises each year equal to the actual rate of inflation.

However, the tax rate has not taken inflation into consideration. Thus, as *The Intellectual Activist* (July 1981) has pointed out, the man who earned $10,000 in 1972 will, in 1984, be paying 63 percent more in taxes on that same inflation-adjusted income. The Reagan administration's tax "break" will not too substantially offset this inflationary disaster.

The meaning of this is very clear. In 1940, a man with an income of $10,000 was doing reasonable well; a man with $30,000 was doing very well indeed. In 1960, for example, a new home of fairly good construction on a larger parcel cost $10,000; that same house sold in 1980, for

$229,000. The people in that neighborhood made $10–15,000 in 1960; in 1980, they made $20–30,000, but the value of their houses had gone up many times more, and their taxes, income and property, were outstripping their income.

Of course, these people seem to be living as well or better, but are they? In 1940 and 1960, these people had very limited debts; now, in the 1980s, they are all disastrously in debt, all overburdened with taxes, and skating on thin ice economically.

They are all taxed as though they were very rich, even while all of them are beginning to feel poorer as their paycheck buys less and less per dollar, and the taxman hits them for a sizable part of their income.

Taxation has become the modern form of slavery. Slavery means ownership in the involuntary labor of another man. All of us work in involuntary servitude to the taxman for about five months every year. This is not freedom, nor is it reasonable.

★ *five* ★

WHAT ARE THE CHURCHES TEACHING?

EARLIER THIS YEAR, a survey of American youth revealed some surprising, as well as disturbing, facts. The Gallup Youth Survey showed that 50 percent of our teenagers attend church or synagogue weekly. The rate of church-going among teenagers is higher than that of adults. Only 40 percent of American adults attend church or synagogue on a weekly basis.

The survey, however, turned up some distressing facts. Although most of the teenagers believe that the Ten Commandments provide valid rules for living, most of them could not say what those rules are. They believed in the Ten Commandments but were not sure what they are!

With respect to the New Testament, three simple questions were asked: Can you name the four Gospels of the New Testament? How many disciples did Jesus have? What religious event or happening is celebrated on Easter? Only 30 percent of all those surveyed answered all three questions correctly. Even those teenagers who went to church regularly flunked this easy test: only 43 percent of them had all three questions correctly answered.

This survey points out some devastating facts. Both the home and the church are failing to provide the religious education in the faith they profess. In fact, it would appear that the church is simply, in all too many cases, babysitting the younger children and entertaining the teenagers. We should not be surprised, therefore, if someone whose parents describe him as a good Sunday-school boy gets involved in serious delinquency. When the church cannot teach the most elementary facts of the faith to its children, it is a failure. Even more, it is irresponsible to society, faithless to God, and generally a detriment to religion.

The question remains, thus, what are the churches teaching? If they cannot pass on the elements of religious knowledge, what justification do they have for their existence? After all, Christ Himself declares:

> Ye are the salt of the earth: but if the salt have lost his savour, wherewith shall it be salted? it is thenceforth good for nothing, but to be cast out, and to be trodden under foot of men. (Matt. 5:13)

It would appear that all too many churches have been ladling out sugar — "sweetness and light" — and have forgotten what it is to be the salt of the earth and to give light to a city.

All freedom is, in essence, a religious fact. It requires us to commit ourselves to a way of life at the price of some other things, and this commitment is inescapably religious. Our freedom today is waning because our faith is lacking, and we are more dedicated to self-interest than to freedom under God.

★ *six* ★

DOES CIVIL GOVERNMENT COST TOO MUCH?

A NUMBER OF years ago, Will Rogers remarked that it was a good thing that we are not getting all the government we are paying for. With that we can agree.

On the other hand, who wants to pay for more government than he wants? We are getting more and more government from federal, state, and local agencies, and the price is getting higher and higher.

According to the Tax Foundation, the cost of all these branches of civil government will exceed $1.007 trillion in 1981. This means the cost to every man, woman, and child is $4,678, or $18,712 for a family of four. You may not pay this all in taxes today, but you will eventually, directly or indirectly.

You may, if you are on welfare, be getting $18,000 in services, but even that is unlikely. One thing is certain: if you work for some agency of civil government, you are indeed ahead of the game. The real beneficiary of statist spending is civil government and nobody else, on the whole.

Moreover, at every level of civil government the budget is prepared by the bureaucracy, and no bureaucracy is prone to cutting its own receipts. In spite of the talk in early and mid-1981 about tax cuts, there were none. All we saw were cuts in the requests for tax increases; with all those supposed tax cuts, we still had our highest budget yet.

We are, in brief, paying more for civil government than we want or get. We are supporting a giant imperial bureaucracy which treats us either as the enemy or as cows to be milked. The main beneficiaries of taxation are not the people but the federal, state, and local agencies of civil government. It is not the people on welfare who are getting rich on our tax money; it is the federal and other levels of government.

When California enacted Proposition 13 and its mandatory cuts on property taxes, the politicians screamed that all kinds of necessary services such as police and fire protection would be cut. None of this happened. Instead, people were less threatened by loss of housing because of heavy taxes, the economy improved, and for most people, the results were overwhelmingly good. Indeed, it became apparent that taxes could have been cut even further, improving the quality of life in California.

Instead of giving us better civil government, our high taxes are giving us oppressive rule, and they are being used to limit and threaten our freedom.

★ *seven* ★

WHO IS CENSORING US?

RECENTLY, *Inquiry* MAGAZINE (August 3, 1981, 24) carried an interesting article by Nat Hentoff on censorship threats. Without agreeing with his thesis, Hentoff's comments were very relevant to the question of film and television censorship.

The fact is that such censorship exists, and it existed before the Moral Majority or Pastor Wildmon's movements were born. A variety of minority groups have long exercised a veto power over what is filmed. Hentoff cites a particularly telling example of an instance of self-censorship in a film production. In the final scene of a film, a key line was cut out for fear of offending "every lesbian in America."

It is obvious that, in any and every film production, a number of forces are at work. Simply in terms of economics, it does not make sense to offend a large segment of the population. A variety of groups exercise a direct and indirect censorship.

This should not surprise us. We are all influences in our speech and action in a particular situation. In certain settings, we inhibit ourselves in order to be better able to function in that place and to accomplish our social goals. Out of good sense, for example, we censor what we say around our boss or around our children. In so doing, we are not cowardly but rather *responsible.*

All too much talk about censorship assumes a social vacuum. The courts have made it clear that to cry fire in a crowded theater is not an exercise of free speech but of irresponsibility. This is an extreme example, but it makes the point. Civil censorship is a dangerous thing;

personal and social censorship can be either good or bad, depending on the circumstances. To express our disapproval of film and television fare is itself an expression of free speech, not of censorship (unless we seek legislation).

Clearly, much of our television fare is stupid, vulgar, and embarrassing to look at. Much of it runs contrary to and is an assault on the moral and religious values of most of us. For most of us, there is little worth watching on television. Now, the producers have the freedom to produce what they want, and we have the freedom to tell them that we think it stinks and to boycott them if we choose. This is what a free society is all about. It means that freedom is a two-way street, and we cannot deny people the freedom to object to what they regard as objectionable if we want the freedom to express ourselves.

★ *eight* ★

ARE PUBLIC SCHOOLS HAZARDOUS TO OUR CHILDREN'S HEALTH?

CIGARETTE SMOKERS FIND on every pack a warning that smoking cigarettes may be hazardous to their health. Now, I am not a smoker, but I rather resent Big Brother's overzealous claim to tell us what is good or bad for us. In my book, that power belongs to God, not the state.

Furthermore, why not a warning on every federal building, reading: "Warning! Big government may be hazardous to your health"? Or why not a notice to every parent of a school child, reading: "Warning! Public schools may be hazardous to your child's health"?

Such a notice would make sense. After all, according to the state of California, in a five-month period, from September 1, 1980, to February 1, 1981, 105,328 incidents of crime and violence at schools were reported. These were crimes against students, teachers, school employees, and property, and included the possession and use of drugs and alcohol, the possession and/or use of weapons, and bomb threats. The property damage in this five-month period came to more than $10.3 million, and the schools had to spend $38.5 million on crime control in the schools.

The figures released dealt with *reported* crimes. Even these tell a grim story. Very obviously, attending a public school today is more hazardous to a child's health than smoking is to adults. Among some of the *unreported* school crimes are shakedowns, compelling children to pay their lunch money as protection money to school bullies or get beaten-up.

More than one teacher has told me that in some schools it can be dangerous for a teacher to turn his or her back on the class. I call that a health hazard.

In fact, why not advertise Washington, D.C., as hazardous to America's health? Paying taxes is not easy on either the pocketbook or your blood pressure. Reading the news from Washington rarely makes me feel happy. Having a federal agent visit me, or asking me to come to his office, I find less desirable than a case of the measles- or worse!

Washington, D.C., makes us all sick at heart much of the time, and after making us sick offers us Medicare! Is there no one up there who still believes that Jefferson was right when he said that the best government is the least government?

After all, the more controls we get, the less freedom we have, and the loss of freedom is very hazardous to the health of a country.

★ *nine* ★

WHO IS MOST HELPED BY FEDERAL SPENDING?

RECENTLY, THOMAS SOWELL, a brilliant economist who is black, called attention to the fact that money taken from the taxpayer to help the poor does not all go to the poor. In fact, Sowell pointed out, every person who is below the poverty line could be lifted above it by *one-third* of the amount actually spent on poverty programs. In the black ghetto of Washington, D.C., the federal government spends almost $46 million but collects $50 million in taxes, so that this ghetto loses $4 million a year on net balance.

What is true of the Washington, D.C., ghetto is true also of the United States as a whole. Whatever the *purpose* of an appropriation, the major *beneficiary* is the federal government. The one thing certain is that when funds are appropriated for any cause, some federal agency will be the main group to prosper.

In at least one city, politicians have spoken against the "high" cost of administration in one or two private charitable organizations. The truth is, that it is the agencies of state whose operating costs are the highest.

In 1890, Mark Hanna wrote a letter of rebuke to a young Republican prosecutor from Ohio, saying, "You have been in politics long enough to know that no man in public office owes the public anything." Since Mark Hanna's day, politicians have learned better than to talk that way. Most of them drip love for the people in their public statements. All too many, however, still act on Mark Hanna's assumption.

The fact remains that the federal government is the main beneficiary of all its programs, not the people. Less and less is it government of, by, and for the people, but more and more, we are getting government of, by, and for the federal bureaucracy.

We once had a remarkable president (this was a long time ago) named James K. Polk. During the 1844 campaign, Polk promised to do five things: acquire Texas and California, settle the Oregon dispute, lower the tariff, establish a subtreasury, and retire from office after four years. He did all those things. He kept his word to the voters, and we have forgotten him! Polk vetoed the use of public money for local and individual interests, and he left office with the treasury highly solvent and on a sound basis.

This does not mean that all Polk's decisions were the best. My point is that Polk worked not to build up the federal power but the freedom and prosperity of the people. He did not promote himself but acted as the people's watchdog. He made the people the beneficiaries of his administration, not the federal power.

Civil government on every level has become too big; it has grown fat on our money and at our expense. It has become a threat to our freedom and a danger to our paycheck. It is time for a change.

★ *ten* ★

HOW DOES THE SUPREME COURT MAKE THOSE DECISIONS?

I HAVE OFTEN wondered how the U.S. Supreme Court can make such strange and far-reaching decisions. The court can take a word or a phrase out of the Constitution and manufacture a whole bureaucracy — full of laws.

Now, I have a sort of theory about the matter. John Marshall was the judge who, early in the Court's history, established its power and its far-reaching interpretations. There is an interesting story about Marshall. In those days, the entire Court stayed at a boarding house while their wives remained in their home states. Since the justices lived together, they discussed the cases all the time, but most seriously at their weekly consultation day in chambers. Some people claimed the justices were drinking too much, so Marshall introduced a rule: no drinking whatsoever on any consultation day, except on those occasions when it was raining. After all, in wet, damp weather, the justices had the right to keep warm!

After a week of sobriety, a consultation day came along, and Marshall was getting thirsty. He asked Justice Joseph Story to go to the window and check on the weather situation. Was there any rain in sight? Story looked one way and then another for some sign of rain, and then came back to the table and said, very earnestly, "Mr. Chief Justice, I have very carefully examined this case. I have to give it as my opinion that there is not the slightest sign of rain." Chief Justice Marshall then delivered his legal verdict: "Justice Story, I think that is the shallowest and most illogical opinion I have ever heard you deliver; you forget that our jurisdiction is as broad as this Republic, and by the laws of nature, it must be raining some place in our jurisdiction. Waiter, bring on the rum."

Well, historians won't agree with me, but I think that kind of thinking is in the background of all too much of the Supreme Court's thinking and much of our law courts.

A man who wants a drink will always come up with a reason for it, and the judge who wants to justify his prejudices will give us Marshall's logic every time! And for this kind of thinking we call them justices!

Marshall's cousin was Thomas Jefferson, and Jefferson said once that if you made any kind of clear-cut statement to Marshall, that he would take your statement, line up legal opinions around it, and prove what you wanted not to believe and he, from the beginning, wanted to conclude. In other words, he made your words a means of embarrassing you! Perhaps that is the reason that many view Marshall as a great judge. Maybe, but not a great champion of freedom.

★ *eleven* ★

ARE FAKE MENACES BEING PROMOTED?

WE ARE REGULARLY told by the press of various cults which are supposedly sweeping the country, capturing countless numbers of youth, fleecing people out of money, and generally creating problems. Among these groups regularly attacked are the Unification Church or "Moonies," the Church of Scientology, and Hare Krishna.

Now, I emphatically disagree with the beliefs of these and other groups, but I strongly disagree with the idea that they are a menace. *First,* in spite of the exaggerated reports about these people, they are numerically small. The "Moonies" in the United States number about 7,000; the Church of Scientology has a membership of between 5,000 and 10,000; the Hare Krishna are about 1,500.

Second, if these or any other groups are out of line, we have more than enough laws on the books to take care of such cases. For example, Jim Jones and the People's Church existed with state and federal cooperation; complaints against the group went unheeded. When the tragedy took place, all kinds of laws were proposed by the people who had done nothing previously. Those new laws would control the rest of us more than the cults.

The same is true today. A number of states are framing legislation to control the "Moonies" and others. These proposed laws are so worded that they would easily control the rest of us.

But this is not all. All too often, the courts have permitted the kidnapping and deprogramming of members of these cults. I would consider it a tragedy if a member of my family joined the "Moonies," but would that make it right for me to have him or her kidnapped? We are now seeing people kidnapped for turning Christian, using the same legal precedents. Will we see people kidnapped in the years ahead for turning Democratic or Republican?

In other words, if we use the law to punish dissent, we are outlawing freedom. A free society requires the possibility of people doing some foolish things. The freedom to make mistakes is an essential part of freedom. While sin is anathema to God, God allows us the option of sinning. He does not alter the fact that sin is sin, but neither does He try to make it impossible for us to sin. What some people are trying to do is to be wiser than God; they want to legislate so as to prevent man from doing anything but the prescribed thing. However well intentioned, such legislation is a stepping-stone to totalitarianism.

Freedom does mean that things we disagree with and even regard as evil can exist, but freedom also means that truth and man alike have an opportunity to grow and develop.

★ *twelve* ★

IS MENTAL ILLNESS A MYTH?

A PROMINENT PSYCHIATRIST, Dr. Thomas Szasz, has for some years upset his fellow practitioners with his studies designed to demonstrate that mental illness is a myth. Much of Dr. Szasz's evidence is very compelling. I do not feel competent to comment on the subject authoritatively, but I would like to suggest that perhaps we have gone overboard on calling a variety of things *mental sickness*. For example, many public school children today supposedly suffer from a disability known as dyslexia, which creates reading problems. When I went to school, we were all taught phonics, and no one had or ever heard of dyslexia. Today, in Christian schools, no one has dyslexia. Perhaps it is real, but we are entitled to some skepticism here.

Another example: in 1850, the Louisiana State Medical Society discovered a new disease — mental disorder — and named it *drapetomania*; "*drapeto*" is a Greek word meaning runaway. The medical commission, headed by a distinguished physician, Dr. Samuel Cartright, found that this disease was a physical and mental peculiarity of the Negro race. The evidence for the medical commission was obvious and clear-cut. A great many Negro slaves were running away. Some of the slave owners from whom they ran away were regarded as fine men. Obviously, running away had to be an indication of some kind of hereditary and racial sickness!

Of course, since the doctors saw nothing wrong with slavery, it did not occur to them that these Negroes were running away from slavery. With equal logic, we can say that a medical degree gives a doctor collection-mania since he has a strong urge to collect on all payments due to him!

Seriously, however, we have gone very much astray on this question of mental illness. We are too prone to label people we disagree with as mentally sick. Is a man politically on the right, left, or center? If so, does that make him a mental case? To be in error is one thing, and to be mentally sick a very different thing.

Implicit in such a labeling is the idea that sick people should be hospitalized and confined. People with erroneous ideas have the same freedom as the rest of us. By labeling those we disagree with as mentally sick, we are implying that freedom should be withdrawn from them. We are then saying that freedom is something to be rationed to our side only. The implications of such labeling are death to freedom.

★ SERIES EIGHT ★

★ *one* ★

DO POLITICIANS LOSE THEIR MEMORY ON ELECTION DAY?

ON FEBRUARY 2, 1970, in London, England, Ronald Reagan made a very astute observation:

> In my country some twenty-five years ago, you could make a long-distance call on a privately owned telephone system from San Francisco to New York for $28. For that same amount of money, you could send 1,376 letters. Today, you can make the same telephone call for two hours and a half and for that amount you can send only 41 letters. So the government is investigating the Bell System![1]

This was an excellent statement, like so many others Reagan made before being elected. The same can be said for the pre-election speeches of Carter, Ford, Nixon, and others before them. It was on March 2, 1930, that candidate Franklin Delano Roosevelt said, "To bring about government by oligarchy masquerading as democracy, it is fundamentally essential that practically all authority and control be centralized in our national government." Roosevelt criticized Hoover for creating a large bureaucracy, and then proceeded to create one so great that Hoover's looked like a hick outfit by comparison.

We are witnessing a growing distrust of politicians because people are finding that representative government is no longer representative. What candidates tell us before election has too little to do with their

---

1 Bill Adler, with Bill Adler, Jr., *The Reagan Wit* (Aurora, IL: Caroline House, 1981), 45.

What candidates tell us before election has too little to do with their behavior after election. Granted, there are exceptions to this, but for the most part, politicians either lose their memory on election day, or else they seem to feel that we, the people, apparently do not mind being sold out again and again.

Crime on the streets is bad—very bad—for society, but I submit that the failure of politicians to keep their word is even worse. It breaks down confidence in the form of civil government, and it leads to a growing contempt for those agencies of law and justice which need respect and support to survive.

Before his election, Mr. Reagan correctly called attention to the difference between telephone rates and postal rates over a twenty-five-year period. In 1981, his first year in office, the postage rate on first-class mail was raised three times, and we heard no comment from the White House. What bothered Candidate Reagan did not bother President Reagan, nor did the fact that rates have gone up while mail service has gone downhill lead to any public statement or action on his part. More than a few people are bothered by this (with good reason), but what troubles me most of all is that plain statements and promises before election day have all too little a relationship to what is done thereafter. The result of all this is a growing disrespect for politicians and the political process, which is a threat to our future.

★ *two* ★

DOES THE UNITED STATES HAVE AN INCURABLE DISEASE?

OUR FOREIGN AID program is one of the strongest aspects of American history. We pour billions of dollars into foreign aid all over the world. Most of this money sticks to the fingers of the politicians in power in the various countries, and some of it is used for strange and unexpected purposes.

I recently learned that Japan uses our aid for defense, then allocates the money they would otherwise use for defense to subsidize their automobile and steel companies, thereby giving them an edge over us.

Now, before you get angry and blame Japan, stop and think for a moment. Being resentful of Japan only makes you a part of the problem. Japan is being sensible — it is taking care of its own interests. If we want to give them money to defend themselves, they are sensible enough to know that their own people and industries are their best defense. Is it any fault of the Japanese that we overtax American workers and auto and steel companies to give Japan money for defense? Why blame Japan and the Japanese for our stupidity? We are, after all, financing our competition all over the world, and we are in some cases helping arm our very enemies.

In other words, why penalize common sense on the part of other nations just because we insist on being idiots?

Clearly, something is wrong with American foreign policy because something is wrong with the United States. Stupidity is a well-nigh incurable condition, and it appears that we have a particularly bad case of it.

Many newspapers, citizens, and politicians do indeed criticize the practices of some countries which receive foreign aid. There is little they can do to change a foreign country, but much they can do to change our own. Perhaps Aesop's fable about the two bags fits us here. Aesop said that every man carries two bags about with him, one in front and one behind, and both are packed full of faults. The bag in front contains our neighbor's faults, and the bag behind contains our own. As a result, we do not see our own faults, only our neighbor's. Well, we cannot change our neighbor, but we can change ourselves by recognizing and dealing with our own faults.

One of our key faults is the mistaken belief that dollars can save the world. Besides being religiously false, this doctrine is clearly a very expensive one. The United States has a humanistic religion of salvation by the dollar rather than by Christ. If we are determined as a nation to hold to some heretical or false religion, why not at least pick a cheaper one? Since World War II, we have spent billions trying to save the world. The world has only gone downhill, and we are facing bankruptcy as a nation.

What is the cause of this condition? Congress and Washington, D.C., seem to think it is more dollars! As for me, I feel that the dollars will do more good in my pocket than in Japan, Kenya, or the Soviet Union.

★ *three* ★

IS OUR BUREAUCRACY BECOMING A BAD JOKE?

EVERY NOW AND then I read about some bureaucratic edict which makes me wonder at the sanity of our uncivil servants. Some time ago, I reported on a case involving a California ski resort. In a chalet on top of the mountain, accessible only by skis, the owners were required to add special toilets for the physically handicapped.

Now, I have read of a case topping even that. I won't mention the city because the many fine people who live there are not responsible for this piece of bureaucratic insanity. A club featuring strip-tease acts was required to build a ramp onto the stage in case any physically handicapped strippers were hired!

Well, I have never attended a strip-tease show, and I certainly never shall. In any case, I most assuredly would not go to see a physically handicapped stripper! How stupid, and insane, do our regulators have to get before we put a stop to this kind of nonsense?

How about some common sense regulations? Why not require seeing-eye dogs for all our legislators, public officials, and bureaucrats, because they obviously cannot see which end is up nor what is ahead of them? Why not require by law every politician to wear a hearing aid so that they can hear us better?

Also, why not ban pensions for all officials, legislators, and bureaucrats *except* those who lower taxes, cut the cost of civil government, and eliminate civil service jobs? Why not a bounty on performance instead of incompetence?

Back to the ramp required by state officials of a strip-tease club: perhaps I have misjudged those fine public servants. Perhaps requiring the ramp is the prelude to requiring handicapped strip-tease dancers. Will the club be forced to become an equal-opportunity employer, hiring the handicapped, the aged, and the ugly for its strip-tease acts?

I have a suggestion to make to these bureaucrats. How can they dare to claim that they are for equal opportunity and fair employment practices when no deaf and dumb persons are hired as radio announcers? Why are no criminals appointed to any supreme court vacancies? Why are the romantic and glamorous parts in films given only to younger women? Do women over eighty have no rights?

If all this sounds crazy, it is simply because what started as a demand for fairness is becoming a bad joke. Facilities for the handicapped make sense in their place, but this does not include a ski lodge nor a strip-tease stage.

How do these bureaucrats get hired anyway? By flunking a sanity test or by giving certifiable evidence of stupidity? It seems that no good law can be passed without being converted into a bad one by the bureaucracy, nor is there any bad law that they cannot succeed in making even worse.

What are they trying to do? To use every law of any kind to increase their power and to limit our freedom?

★ *four* ★

DO OUR EX-PRESIDENTS COST TOO MUCH?

ONE OF THE very substantial drains on taxpayers is paying for ex-legislators and bureaucrats. This includes the high price of ex-presidents. Each ex-president receives an annual pension of $69,630. This, however, is only the tip of the iceberg. For the first thirty months after leaving office, the ex-president is entitled to an office staff with an aggregate salary ceiling of $150,000 per year; after the thirty months, this drops to $96,000 per year. On top of this, the taxpayer pays for office facilities. Nixon's office in Manhattan cost $60,000 a year; Ford's, in Palm Springs, California, costs $54,573 a year; Carter's, in Atlanta, cost about $340,000, and Carter also rents an office in his mother's home in Plains, Georgia, for $250 a month. Add to this for all these men, various decorating costs, moving costs, the cost of office supplies, newspapers and periodicals, office plants and watering and fertilizing services for the plants in Ford's offices, as well as cable television — and no postage costs. This list does not cover all items.

Of course, the men get Secret Service protection as well. The cost of the Secret Service protection is about $8.5 million per year, so we are talking about a large staff of men. Then the presidential libraries housing their papers and other items cost, according to *Inquiry* magazine (November 23, 1981), about $12.5 million a year.

All this does not compare to the cost of the presidency, which rises with each man. Our presidents now live better than royalty ever lived.

The visible cost of the White House for 1982 is $26 million, but vast amounts are and have been charged off to national defense and a variety of other accounts, as Bill Gulley, in *Breaking Cover*, made clear. So great and hidden is the cost of our new royalty that Clark Norton, in *Inquiry* ("Royalty Payments") says, "Perhaps most disturbing of all is the simple fact that while the cost of the presidency has grown to staggering proportions, no one has the foggiest idea of the total expenditures."

Promises of economy are a joke. Carter promised to cut the White House staff and practice economy. He did cut the official staff nearly 30 percent, but he transferred over seventy employees to another agency while continuing to use them and others, so that his actual staff was 30 percent larger than Ford's. All our presidents have played games like this with us, and for this we reward them handsomely. Of course, it is Congress that does the rewarding, and why not? What president will object when Congress gives itself like benefits and that president knows he will get more of the same?

In other words, government is less and less of, by, and for the people, but of, by, and for the bureaucracy and the politicians. They get the benefits, and we get the bill. There is some justice to all this: whether we are Republicans or Democrats, this is what we keep voting for. Most people are only trying to get in line for their share of the handout. In the process, our form of government and our freedom are suffering badly.

★ *five* ★

MUST CIVIL GOVERNMENT HAVE A DOUBLE STANDARD?

ALL OF US are faced annually with deadlines from one agency of the federal or state governments: a deadline for filing state and federal income tax returns and payments; property tax deadlines; car license deadlines; business deadlines, and so on. If we are tardy in filing, we pay a penalty. This is as it should be. The orderly conduct of life and business requires deadlines and penalties, and I am not about to suggest abandoning them. On the contrary, I want them extended to include every agency of state.

Let me illustrate. A friend had to make very large withholding payments on his income tax in the first half of one year, and he then made almost nothing in the second half. As a result, he had $5,000 coming to him, which he needed badly. Of course, he waited a couple of years for it, and in the process, he was audited before he was repaid.

Or take this case. When a driveway was being built which entered a state highway, the highway department required that a $1,000 bond be posted, to be returned when the work was completed and approved. However, when the work was finished and approved, the state highway department made no haste to return the money. After a telephone call, it was promised by the first of the month, but the first of that coming month and the next passed without any check arriving.

In one city, several small contractors suffered bad credit ratings and near-bankruptcy after working on a federal project. Almost a year later, they were still awaiting payment and were all in financial trouble.

Of course, if you and I are late on any of our tax payments, we are penalized. Quite obviously, there is a double standard at work here.

All these federal and state agencies claim that the problem is that they are overworked. How about the rest of us? Are we not overworked filling out their forms on top of doing our own work? Moreover, no one has a higher percentage of help per volume of work than does a bureaucracy.

A friend of mine pays between $50,000 and $100,000 a year in one form of tax after another on his business. His one secretary handles all the organization's telephone and secretarial work. This man, as a good accountant, spends much time every workweek keeping accounts and filling out forms for the taxman.

There is so much bookwork required of persons and businesses that accounting has become a major growth industry. Some small Western counties have more accountants than they do policemen and sheriff's deputies, and this may well be true of the big cities as well. We need the policemen to protect us from hoodlums, but we Americans need as many or more accountants to protect us from the state and federal governments. Are we getting our money's worth from either the state capitol or Washington, D.C.?

★ *six* ★

DO WE HAVE EQUAL JUSTICE?

ON OCTOBER 1, 1981, the Equal Access to Justice Act went into effect. After many years of effort by small businesses, this measure was finally passed by Congress. Certainly, there were some serious evils that needed correcting. The federal bureaucracy could take a businessman to court and, even if the businessman won his case, put him through the wringer or into bankruptcy because of legal expenses.

For example, a restaurant owner in Tulsa, Oklahoma, in a Labor Department case, refused to settle for $15,000 in fines. He fought the case and was vindicated, but his legal costs were over $30,000. A furniture manufacturer in Missouri fought a charge and finally won, but his attorneys' fees were several times the net worth of his factory. A woman in a small Pennsylvania town won a case against a federal agency, but her new business went under because of the heavy costs and the long legal delays.

The Equal Access to Justice Act requires the federal government to reimburse the legal fees and court costs of small businesses *and* individuals who prevail in civil cases with federal agencies. This act is a step in the right directions, but some very serious problems still remain.

First, how can anyone be compensated for two to four years or more of a legal battle for survival? It involves costs other than legal fees, such as financial and emotional costs, which can run high. Five and ten years after such a battle, the scars and costs are still there. *Second*, the persons who really pay the legal fees and the court costs are the businesses and individuals who win the case; they pay it in the form of taxes. The losing bureaucrats do not pay it out of their own pockets; they are not in the least penalized for having brought a wrongful action against someone. On the contrary, since they have nothing to lose, they on occasion punish the winning citizen by going after him again.

Even when we win and our court costs and legal fees are reimbursed to us, we are the losers because of the cost of time and the vulnerability to more attacks. When the state or the federal government loses, it bills us for the cost of our victory in the form of taxes.

In other words, one way or another, the state and the federal government turn everything into a game of Russian roulette — one in which the gun is always at our heads, and they load the gun and pull the trigger.

We do not have equal justice. Our courts are state and federal courts, and promotion or advancement for judges comes by pleasing the powers of the state. Most of the cases heard by the U.S. Supreme Court are heard on appeal from some agency or officer of the state or federal governments. The Equal Access to Justice Act of 1981 was indeed a step in the right direction, but we need several more stages, and a mile or two, to rectify the imbalance in justice.

★ *seven* ★

HOW SERIOUSLY SHOULD WE TAKE OUR POLITICIANS?

WHENEVER THE DEMOCRATS are in office, the Republicans start to wail for the future of the people. We the people are being forgotten by the Democratic "fat-cats," and only they have the welfare of the people at heart. When the Republicans are in office, we get the same song and the same kind of tears from the Democrats. With two such great and powerful parties manifesting a bleeding heart for us, the people, we should by now be at the gates of paradise. The sad fact, however, is that politicians of all stripes get richer and fatter at our expense, and we the people are worse off. Go abroad and the same thing holds true. Foreign socialist, communist, and fascist parties are all for the people, but somehow, the people are usually the losers.

The Japanese have an old proverb which tells us why this is so. The proverb declares, "When the cat mourns for the mouse, do not take her seriously." The political fat-cats of all stripes and colors are always mourning for the mice — after they devour them. If you take them seriously, you will be their victim.

If you believe that political parties are going to do anything but help themselves into power, you belong on the honor roll of All-American pigeons. No doubt, you will also believe that cattlemen can become a lobby for vegetarianism or that deer hunters look back on *Bambi* as their all-time favorite movie.

The fact is that "where there are fish, there must be water" (Japanese proverb), and where there are politicians, there is a quest for power—power over us. To forget that is dangerous. We can be grateful for one thing: politicians are not immortal, and the judgment of God is above and over them. As the Russian proverb states, "The greatest king must, at last, be put to bed with a shovel."

Meanwhile, you and I need to be cured of a very bad "bug": the belief in salvation by politics. Because, in the past few years, men have actually believed that Kennedy, Johnson, Nixon, Ford, Carter, and Reagan could solve our problems and give us a better life, we are in a mess. Our ex-presidents, ex-senators, ex-congressmen, ex-governors, and so on are doing very well indeed, but with all the years of progress they have brought us, why am I having more trouble paying my bills? Why am I having a problem trying to figure out how I can buy my next used car? Why do I feel less free than I did twenty years ago?

Politicians have good answers for making their political parties and themselves more powerful and richer, but those plans are at your expense and mine.

★ *eight* ★

IS DISCRIMINATION ALWAYS BAD?

ACCORDING TO *The Intellectual Activist* (October 1, 1981), a district court judge in late 1981 ruled that an applicant's psychosis is not a lawful ground for a medical school to deny admission. A young woman entered a university medical school without disclosing her previous psychiatric hospitalization. As a student there, she did such things as cutting herself to cause bleeding and physically assaulting doctors. The school required her to take a leave of absence, and during that time she was again hospitalized. She was later denied her application for readmission to the medical school, and she sued the school under the Rehabilitation Act of 1973. The court ruled in her favor.

Is it not time that we recognize that discrimination can be both good and bad? Would it make sense, for example, to allow a paroled rapist to be a teacher in a girls' school? Would a paroled bank robber make a good teller?

Certainly, a man or woman's past record should not be held against him or her, but neither can it be disregarded. An opportunity for rehabilitation is important, but it must be a sensible opportunity. To make a former drug addict the person in charge of a hospital's drug supply is not being fair either to the hospital or the ex-junkie. There is a difference between opportunity and stupidity, and between justice and injustice. In the name of no discrimination we can unjustly impose upon the public a person they would choose not to have if they knew the facts.

Perhaps there were mitigating circumstances in the medical-school case, and perhaps there were not. I simply do not know. What I do know is that the Rehabilitation Act of 1973 ignores the realities of situations and imposes a straitjacket upon institutions and the public.

Discrimination is not necessarily bad nor necessarily good; it can be either, depending upon the circumstances. If I discriminate against someone because of his or her nationality or color, I am depersonalizing him or her and am wrong. If I discriminate against him or her because I have found him or her to be morally untrustworthy and financially dishonest, I am being both right and sensible.

The law, however, says that no program, agency, or institution can exercise common-sense discrimination if it is receiving federal financial assistance. Medical and other schools receive such assistance, as do a variety of other institutions. Should your local public school have no right to discriminate against certain types of individuals with known records, in hiring teachers and employees? Should a paroled poisoner have the right to a job in a school lunch room or kitchen? What happens to *our* freedom under such a law?

★ *nine* ★

IS THERE A GOOD EXCUSE FOR MURDER?

IN DECEMBER 1981, two women were released in Britain after trials, one for threatening to kill a police officer, the other after killing a man. The twenty-nine-year-old barmaid, who threatened a policeman's life while carrying a knife, had thirty previous convictions for arson and assault and was on probation for stabbing to death another barmaid in the previous year. The other woman, aged thirty-seven, had driven her car into her lover after an argument in December 1980.

Both women gained release because their attorneys pleaded that PMT, not the women, was responsible. PMT is premenstrual tension. It has now gained a standing as a defense against criminal charges.

This can be scary news for both men and women. If a woman can walk out of court free after murdering a man, pleading pre-menstrual tension, any angry woman has a license to kill and make use of this plea. It could become risky for a man to disagree with his wife when such a convenient legal excuse for murder is provided. Hopefully, this legal plea may not succeed in the United States, but you can be sure some lawyers will use it soon. We already have all too many similarly inane pleas being successfully used.

What such decisions as these two in Britain do is to strike at the foundations of morality, law, and freedom. The Biblical foundation of Western law insists on man's responsibility and accountability for his actions. This accountability is to both God and man, and there are no valid excuses for sin nor crime. Premenstrual tensions can be a problem, as can migraine headaches. Trouble with our boss, fellow worker, or employee can make us frantic. Then, too, most wives and husbands can be very aggravating at times. The whole point of morality is that, given these aggravations and given the sinful nature of our being, we conform ourselves to moral law, not our hatreds, frustrations, and aggravations. To justify a crime because of aggravations is to reward precisely the evil or the worst side of our being, whereas the point of law and morality is that evil is punished and moral conduct is protected.

The barmaid who was freed had thirty previous convictions, including a killing, all by the age of twenty-seven. Very obviously, she had not served much time in prison to have a record which included a killing, arson, and assault by the age of twenty-seven.

What such records tell us is that we are soft on crime and hard on the victims. They tell us that, throughout the Western world, lawlessness is flourishing, law-abiding citizens are being hurt badly, and the law is not concerned. If a woman can deliberately run her car over her lover and kill him, and then walk out of the courtroom on a plea of premenstrual tension, then why bother to have any laws against killing?

★ *ten* ★

CAN WE LEGISLATE OUR WAY INTO PARADISE?

I READ A glowing report on the decisions made by the twenty-sixth congress of the CPSU in the Soviet Union. The report cited the following measures taken to create a marvelous society in the next few years.

Over sixteen billion roubles have been appropriated in the Five-Year Plan for increased wages, salaries, and other benefits. The report states, "Comparatively speaking, these payments are enough to build ten cities, each with a population of one million, or a score of hydroelectric power stations of the Nourek size." The plan calls for building 530 to 540 million square meters of housing to house fifty million people, nine billion roubles for state allowances to families, and an additional ten billion roubles for wage and salary increases in 1985. Nursery school buildings will be enlarged to care for three million more children. Grain production is to be increased by 238 to 243 million tons, and meat production by more than three million tons. It is also a part of the plan to increase the Soviet Union's national income by 18 to 20 percent, according to the Five-Year Plan.

All this sounds very impressive, but it means very little. We know a great deal, for example, about the grain production. Each successive Five-Year Plan has promised a substantial increase, but with little or no results and sometimes negative results. Without foreign grain, the people of the Soviet Union would face famine and starvation. This is a particularly significant fact because, prior to the revolution and World

War I, the Ukraine was Europe's breadbasket. The grain and food situation was then a good one, and ever since, it has been an increasingly bad one.

Moreover, at one time, not too many years ago, the peasants on the collective farms grew on their private garden plots and sold on the black market about 50 percent of the internal Soviet food supply. Now that production is down to 30 percent because the younger workers have no desire to work.

Thus, all the Five-Year Plans are exercises in futility. Their net impact has been to produce reams of dishonest statistics from bureaucrats who refuse to admit that the plans have failed. Still, they continue because of a religious faith in man and man's planning rather than in God and freedom under God.

The Soviet Union is a dramatic illustration of the fact that planning is no substitute for freedom, and it will not work. With such examples as the Soviet Union, Red China, and other disasters of statist planning, one would think we would show better sense than to trust in planners and their plans. Legislation is never a valid substitute for faith, character, and freedom. Our future as a country requires us to return to those standards which alone create the faith and life which makes for freedom, productivity, and peace.

★ *eleven* ★

IS BEING HUMAN A DISASTER?

I READ A book review which saddened me. The book is by a very able and charming writer, but all his charm cannot conceal his radical emptiness because he has no faith.

The book reviewer's title for his review is, "The Disaster of Being a Human Being." The author's basis for such cynicism is stated by a character who says, "The atheists are right. There is no justice, no Judge. There is no one ruling the world." What, then, are we to do? What is the author's answer? Two sentences sum it up: "As long as you breathe, you must breathe . . . One should always be joyous." Well, this is better counsel than the suicidal verdicts of others, but still none too good. If life has no meaning and being human is a disaster, why then breathe, and what is there to be joyous about?

I am inclined to think that they who claim that God is dead and life is meaningless are like the modern educators, who, according to C. S. Lewis, geld a man and then bid him be fruitful. We can also compare it to chopping down a tree and then expecting a harvest from it next summer.

As Richard Weaver told us some years ago, ideas have consequences. If we insist that being human is a disaster, we shall certainly make ourselves into walking disasters and the world into a disaster area, which is what we have done. If we declare that God is dead and His moral law dead also, should we be surprised if we are not soon like moral zombies — the living dead?

In terms of material benefits, conveniences of living, life expectancy, educational possibilities, and much, much more, man has never been better off than we in this country are today. In terms of faith, morality, and law, we are a disaster.

All too many people view today and tomorrow with little or no hope. Now, hope is one of the greatest psychic nourishments and enticements possible for man. Without hope, a man has no future. One of our most prolific industries today is the proclamation of hopelessness. Our press, literature, and films all too often reek with a sense of hopelessness. Such people are insisting that the world is as small as they are. A popular book of a few years ago was titled, very wisely, *Your God Is Too Small.* A sequel could be written as to how small we have made our world by our thinking. In the old days of Saturday movie serials, one frequent horror scene had the hero or heroine trapped in a cell with spiked walls which then began to close in on him or her. Too many of our contemporary authors write as though they were trapped, and all mankind with them, in a narrow cell with the walls closing in to destroy them.

But don't you believe it! This is still God's world, and freedom under God is our calling.

★ *twelve* ★

IS CHARITY ILLEGAL?

MOST OF US saw, on television news, the give-away program in Oakland, California, where 500,000 pounds of oranges were given away in late 1981 by farmer Skip Pescosalido of Exater, California. All he asked was the cost of freight and packing, and the West Oakland Food Co-op asked recipients to donate two cents per orange to defray expenses.

Because of this, Pescosalido has become the target of a federal lawsuit. He may be fined $150,000 and assessed an additional $16,000. Federal agents have already spent 500 hours going over his business records, and the worst may be ahead for him. Perhaps some political decision may lead to no prosecution, but this is far from sure.

All this is based on a 1937 U.S. Department of Agriculture order creating a Navel Orange Administrative Committee. This committee determines the number of navel oranges that growers can ship to the market. The 1981 order limited California and Arizona growers to shipping only 76 to 78 percent of the oranges grown to the market. The rest had to be exported, made into juice, or fed to cattle. In 1981, according to Pescosalido, 26,872,000 boxes were diverted to nonhuman use — dumped in pastures for cows to walk on.

There are two important issues in this case. *First,* does a man have the right to sell his produce where and however he wants it? Does the federal government have the right to limit the amount of produce that goes to the market? The federal government has been exercising such a power since the days of President Roosevelt.

Second, does the federal government have the right to tell us when we can be charitable and when we cannot be? There were no complaints from the people of Oakland who received the oranges.

We can raise still a *third* question. Is federal planning and control a superior force to freedom and the free market? Pescosalido's critics seem to believe that the consequence of freedom is a disaster; they maintain that the free market would destroy. Pescosalido charges, in turn, that such critics — both farmers and nonfarmers — are either members of a major distributing corporation or federal officials.

The issue is an important one. In the Pescosalido case, freedom is on trial. All too many people, both in and out of the federal government, seem to believe that freedom is a potentially dangerous force and (if permitted at all) should be very strictly rationed. Whatever the decision in the Pescosalido case, this issue will remain key in the last two decades of the twentieth century.

★ *thirteen* ★

WHEN IS IT ILLEGAL TO SING IN CHURCH?

IN 1981, A public high school in a Midwestern state had to stop scheduling appearances by the school chorus in religious institutions. The school board was threatened with court action unless it put a stop to all such concerts. The school board, given the hostility of the courts to all such things, indicated that it would comply with the demand, and no more concerts would be held in churches or synagogues (*The Presbyterian Journal*, November 4, 1981, 3).

One of the problems for music directors in high schools is finding an audience for their choruses. All year long, the students learn and rehearse, but the singing opportunities are few. One of the best incentives to the students, however, is an appearance before a group of adults. In many areas, churches have provided an excellent opportunity. Each year, churches have a number of midweek activities such as a mother and daughter banquet, a father and son dinner, a harvest festival, and so on. These occasions have kept many a high-school chorus both busy and happy, and they have been excellent means of public relations. Now they are forbidden.

Now, in the name of the First Amendment, they are forbidden. Why? How do they violate the First Amendment?

The First Amendment has two aspects. *First*, it stipulates that there can be no establishment of any particular religious organization. Establishment historically has meant the state financing and governing of a particular church. How did these choir appearances constitute establishment? The main beneficiary has always been the high-school chorus, which receives an audience.

Second, the First Amendment bars the civil authorities from infringing on the free exercise of religion. How can anyone say that a high-school chorus singing at a church's harvest festival has somehow prevented the free exercise of religion?

This, however, is the kind of "law" we are getting. Is it any wonder that all our First Amendment guarantees are steadily being diminished by reinterpretation?

The high-school choruses lost a major audience because of this step. However, all of us become losers because the law was used to achieve unreasonable ends and to further the demolition of law and society. Legal irrationality is increasingly the order of the day and a major force for irrationality and disorder in life.

★ SERIES NINE ★

★ *one* ★

IS LANGUAGE A POLITICAL TOOL?

LANGUAGE IS INCREASINGLY used by politicians to obscure rather than to convey meaning. Any resemblance between campaign promises and election performances is purely coincidental. Our present and immediately past presidents were good in their promises and very different in their actions.

Now we have a new piece of wisdom from Governor Jerry Brown of California, a candidate for the U.S. Senate this year (1982). According to *The Intellectual Activist* (December 1, 1981), he has come up with this pearl of wisdom: "The trouble with drunk driving laws is that drunk and sober are metaphysical concepts."

The concern of metaphysics is with questions of ultimate reality; so, understood from this perspective, drunk and sober means, for most of us, that there are real facts. But Jerry Brown, who dabbles in Zen Buddhism, believes that the ultimate reality is nothingness, so that for him "drunk" and "sober" are empty words in a vast cosmos of meaninglessness.

Jerry Brown is a more consistently religious man than most politicians, and so he speaks here with a clarity and an honesty. From his religious perspective, words are merely terms for ephemeral and meaningless phenomena.

Most of us, however, view and use words from a framework governed by the Bible. We thus do not see words, nor the things they represent, as meaningless. Rather, for us communication depends on the reality of meaning; both words and what they stand for are important and real for us.

Our problem is that, in the politics of the modern state, a different religious perspective lurks behind the scenes, and the old meanings we treasure are meaningless to the politicians.

This, of course, is the world of George Orwell's *1984*—the world of Doublethink and Newspeak.

We have, for example, been assured at one time or another by both Republicans and Democrats that a budget deficit can be a good thing. How many of us who run into a deficit situation before our next paycheck find it a good situation to be in? Does politics sanctify insanity and nonsense?

If our politicians misuse language so easily and casually, perhaps it is because most of us do so also. If I am not a man of my word, nor are you, and we will hardly vote for a man who is. We will feel more comfortable with someone who is careless with the truth if we ourselves are also.

We need politicians with integrity in their hearts and their words, but to have such men, we the people must also have integrity.

★ *two* ★

HOW FRIENDLY ARE YOU TO VAMPIRES?

WE HAVE A very sensitive and thoughtful federal government these days, some would say. After all, the Equal Employment Opportunity Commission has spent a few years receiving about 150 cases in which people claimed they were vampires and were being discriminated against because of their nature and their birthplace in Transylvania (*Reason*, April 1982, 10). According to *Reason Magazine*, former EEOC vice-chairman Dan Leach says that the agency's staff members were "so mindless and overzealous that, instead of immediately tossing the vampires' charges out, they let them get as far as preliminary examinations." Now the vampires have had it: their cases will no longer be considered.

Perhaps this is a sign of a returning sanity in our federal government, but it is premature to say so. Our bureaucracy and our courts still continue to strain gnats and swallow camels with their normal lack of common sense. Perhaps the only thing keeping these 150 vampires out of the courts is a lack of money!

After all, the U.S. Supreme Court, in the case of *Eddings v. Oklahoma*, overturned the death sentence of a young man who shot and killed a highway patrolman who stopped him. The Court gave as its reason the failure of the lower court to consider the criminal's background of broken homes (*The Intellectual Activist*, December 1, 1981). If a broken home is an excuse for murder, then, with all the broken homes in America, a very great number of licenses for murder have been issued by the U.S. Supreme Court.

I hope, like me, that you are thoroughly fed up with all this nonsense. A bureaucracy and courts concerned with such absurdities as the rights of vampires and excuses for murder are no longer serving the interests of the people nor of justice. Our federal and state governments get more bloated each year, more arrogant, and less and less rational. The bigger civil government becomes, the more uncivil, irrational, and absurd it becomes.

Washington, D.C., and the federal government have finally stopped processing vampire cases, but I do wish the federal government would stop playing vampire with us. Taxes are becoming a blood-sucking operation, and at least one Washington observer believes that all our local, state, and federal taxes, direct and indirect, now total over half our income. It used to be that we worked into late May just to pay our taxes; now it is into July.

I don't believe in Transylvanian vampires, but I am beginning to realize we have our homegrown varieties in Washington, D.C., and in our state capitols, and it does hurt to feed a vampire!

We cannot long have freedom with a power state that overtaxes and over-controls the people. Basic to freedom is a strong people and a less strong civil government. Our freedom today is threatened, not simply from abroad, but especially from here at home by a power-hungry civil government, a vast bureaucracy, and a mindless judiciary. Our civil government is no substitute for freedom.

★ *three* ★

HOW BIG ARE THE BIG CORPORATIONS?

WE HEAR A great deal of talk these days about the menace of big corporations and statements about how big they are. Are these statements true?

Now, I am not a friend of corporations; in fact, I have just wound up a loser in a battle with an insurance company, and it has left me wound up and mad. However, the Bible makes it clear that we must tell the truth about someone irrespective of our personal feelings.

Michael Novack has recently given some data on the 500 largest industrial corporations in America. The largest of these is General Motors, with more than 200 units; its largest branch in Michigan employs, at peak, no more than 14,000 people. In 1979, General Motors was much better off than it is now, and its total number of employees was 839,000. In Washington, D.C., the executive branch of the federal government, in that same year, listed 2,806,513 employees, and the Department of Defense, 971,968. On top of that, General Motors is much larger than most of the 500 big corporations: more than twice as big as General Electric and almost five times as big as U.S. Steel, one of the biggest corporations.

The smallest of the 500 largest corporations has only 529 employees. In other words, no corporation compares with our biggest federal agencies, and some are quite small in reality. Most of our bigger corporations are closer in size to a big university system, such as the University of California.

But this is not all. In 1979, General Motors had to pay out in interest on loans ninety-three cents of every dollar of net profit; this means that General Motors was and is in a very shaky financial situation. To varying degrees, this same bad financial outlook was faced in 1979 (and is worse now) by all of the big 500 corporations save one smaller one.

How big are the big corporations? Not very big indeed. If you put a handful of the biggest federal agencies together, you will far outweigh in money and manpower all 500 of the biggest corporations.

Where bigness is concerned, our problem is in Washington, D.C., and the federal government. Our problem is not big business and big labor, but big government on city, county, state, and federal levels. This does not mean that we do not have problems with some big businesses and big banking. For one thing, they are on the whole gutless when it comes to fighting big government, especially on the federal level.

My point is that we have been fed a line about bigness. We have been looking in the wrong direction as to the nature of our problem. The federal government creates inflation by deficit spending, but the corner grocery store and the power company get the blame for raising prices when they are simply trying to keep pace with inflation. When I was quite young, haircuts were twenty-five cents; my last one cost me $4. The barber, like the grocer, the service station, and the power company, is simply reflecting the fact of inflation. He did not make it; inflation is made in Washington, D.C., and exported everywhere.

Bigness is indeed a problem, but it is the bigness of the federal government which is threatening all of us.

★ *four* ★

WHAT IS A MONOPOLY?

ANY ORGANIZATION OR institution which has exclusive control over an area of life or the economy is a monopoly. No monopoly can really exist without statist protection to eliminate competition. A monopoly is thus a state-created power over a section of our life or economy. At one time, a state-established church had a monopoly on religion, but monopolies now tend to lie in other areas.

In some cities, we have a monopoly by a taxi company; the city refuses to license any other cab company. Two other common monopolies are telephone and power. These are limited monopolies, as are cab companies. If you don't like the taxi, you can still take the bus or drive your car. An electrical power company has a state license or granted monopoly, but its control is still limited.

For example, our regional power company made a blunder during the energy crisis, as did most power companies. It assumed that the price of oil would continue to climb sharply, and so it signed a long-term contract at price rises more gradual than it estimated would take place. In 1981, Congress deregulated oil to a degree, and the price first rose and then dropped as free-market supply and demand took over. However, for the power companies, the price rose in terms of their contract commitment.

Our power bill doubled in one month. Everyone in our area was angry. People began to turn off the heat, use their fireplaces, wear long johns and warmer clothing, and to cut their fuel usage in every way possible. My own power bill, for a very cold winter month, dropped to a seven-year low. The power company was hurt, and it quickly promised the strictest measures to give us lower rates.

Thus, although I have only one power company to choose from, I can limit my use of its services. I *cannot* do this with any level of civil government. It is impossible for me to tell the Internal Revenue Service that I do not intend to use any of a number of federal services and to deduct a portion of my tax bill, without having to face a court. I cannot tell the state or county that I am against their road expansion and development program and then deduct a given portion of my tax bill.

In other words, the modern power state — "big government" — is our one true monopoly. The more the federal government grows, the greater its monopolistic control over all of us.

Basic to a monopoly is its power to eliminate the fact of *choice*. Now, choice is basic to freedom. Choice means that I can choose my place of residence, my job, my wife, my friends and associates, and I can go and come, stay or move, at my option. It is the essence of the Marxist monopoly-states that one after another, many of these choices are infringed. Even the freedom of a Russian girl to marry an American boy is controlled.

The United States is by no means a monopoly-state on the same level as Red China or the Soviet Union, but with each new bigger budget and the steady growth of the federal and state governments, we move a step closer to being the same kind of monopoly.

Monopoly as a parlor game may be fine, but as a fact of life, it is dangerous to freedom. Bigness in civil government is the most deadly form of bigness and monopoly.

★ *five* ★

WILL OUR COURTS DEFEND ORPHANS?

AN OLD STORY, which may or may not be true, tells of a man who murdered both his father and his mother, and then asked the judge to show mercy on the grounds that he was an orphan!

Well, that kind of gall is all too commonplace today. As a matter of fact, some men who had murdered their parents were claiming and getting Social Security survivor's benefit checks. This kind of drain on Social Security was ended in January 1982, when newspapers publicly called attention to two glaring cases of such benefits. One such murderer collected $21,500 on parole; another collected about $8,000 in survivor's benefits. That, however, has been stopped by the federal government, at least for the time being. If some claimant goes to court demanding survivor's benefits for Social Security after murdering his or her parents, our courts have proven that they are silly enough to hear such arguments.

Everyone has their day in court these days, sometimes at taxpayers' expense, except the taxpayer. He is too busy earning a living and paying his taxes to have the time or the money to go to court.

However, we can comfort ourselves with the thought that, last year, some Social Security money did go to orphans who murdered their parents. Our tax money went into publishing pamphlets being distributed by the Federal Consumer Information Center. From that agency you can order such important literature as, "Dennis the Menace: Coping with Family Stress," or "How to Adopt a Wild Horse or Burro." Now, all you folks who want a wild horse or burro in your home should feel grateful that Washington is thinking of you, at your expense, of course. Come to think of it, I would be very happy to think of you for the same kind of money!

Well, I shouldn't be sarcastic. After all, the federal government is very thoughtful and concerned about all of us. To keep us from doing foolish things, it takes away a big chunk of our money each year, which is downright thoughtful and neighborly. But this is not all. According to an old saying, in the spring, a young man's fancy turns lightly to thoughts of love; for that matter, a middle-aged or older man can get a little too fanciful in the spring. Our thoughtful federal government keeps us men from making fools of ourselves. From December 31 to April 15, the Internal Revenue Service keeps us so busy trying, first, to figure out our taxes, and, second, how to pay them and still eat, that spring comes and goes before we have a chance for foolish thoughts or actions.

Meanwhile, at any rate, HHS Secretary Richard Schweiker has halted the previous policy of allowing people who murder their parents to collect survivor's benefits on parole. Hopefully, if the courts do not interfere, Schweiker's decision will stand. Let us hope that no agency or committee begins an investigation of Schweiker for showing too much sanity in government. After all, too many more decisions like Schweiker's and people will expect sanity everywhere in the federal government. Then the whole Potomac operation will go down the tubes.

★ *six* ★

HOW MUCH ARE FEDERAL REGULATIONS COSTING US?

ACCORDING TO MURRAY Weidenbaum, chairman of the Council of Economic Advisors, the cost of federal regulations to U.S. consumers in 1980 was $126 billion. In 1976, it was $100 billion. Thus, in four years, the cost of regulations went up over 25 percent. According to Weidenbaum, his figure of $126 billion is a conservative estimate (*Reason*, April 1982, 18).

These regulations do not come cheaply. They cost every man, woman, and child about $570 a year, or $22,000 a year for a family of four. This is a very substantial tax on all of us.

Now, let us grant that some regulation might be called necessary. However, given the prodigal and wasteful character of the federal government, we can safely assume that even the best of regulations are neither wisely nor economically administered. We can also be reasonably certain that we are often unwisely and ineptly overregulated in many other areas, as well as overregulated where we need no regulations at all.

After all, this country began, grew, and became great and powerful on the premise that, in virtually every area of life, the best regulatory power is freedom itself. The fact is, freedom does regulate us all. It requires us to be responsible, aware of consequences, and ready to live with our decisions.

Some years ago, an immigrant woman from Northern Europe told me of her experience on landing in the United States. She came from a very conservative and highly protective community. She had never made any decisions on her own; first her family and then her husband made them all for her. On her first full day in the United States, her husband went off to look for work, and she heard a knock on the door. It was a door-to-door salesman selling sewing machines. She had never said no to a man before in her life; she had been protected at every turn and never made a decision. As a result, before she was fully aware of it, she had signed a contract to make weekly payments for some time to come. When her husband came home and heard her tearful story, he said, "Well, girl, this is America, and a free country. You had better grow up fast." She laughed as she told me that she grew up overnight, learned how to be critical, and how to say no. For years, she occasionally patted the old sewing machine and called it her university education.

Within limits, freedom does educate, and regulations overprotect us. Old-fashioned rugged individualism was at times very irresponsible, but new-fashioned overregulation is no less reprehensible and often much worse for the American character.

Our present state of overregulation is costing us too much money, but it is also exacting a high price in character and in freedom. Basic to the present philosophy of regulations is the belief that the people cannot be trusted with freedom, that freedom is dangerous and much too conducive to public and private immorality, and that freedom itself must be licensed, limited, and rationed. As a result, we are turning our backs on the very thing that made the United States a great power: the love of freedom.

★ *seven* ★

IS FREEDOM DANGEROUS?

IN THIS CENTURY, we have seen a dramatic change in American life. From a strong affirmation of freedom as a necessary and moral fact, we have turned rather steadily to a distrust of freedom and a belief in regulations.

Is this faith in the health and virtue of regulations and controls justified? In certain areas of life, we all tend to believe in regulations. We do *not* believe that a man should have the freedom to shout "Fire!" in a crowed theater. We do *not* believe that an eight-year-old child should have the freedom to drive a car. We do *not* believe that a murderer should be turned loose and have his freedom at will.

Obviously, we place some very serious restrictions on freedom, even to the point of imprisonment or execution in some cases. However, our restrictions on freedom have historically had a common factor. We have held to the premise that an irresponsible person should not have freedom, particularly if his activities can or have endangered or destroyed the lives of others. As a result, none of us have the right to shout "Fire!" in a crowded theater. To do so is dangerously irresponsible.

The common fact in the limitation of freedom is this factor: irresponsibility which can be a menace to the lives and persons of others. We therefore control minors and limit their freedom; we also limit the freedom of convicted criminals because they have used their freedom to the injury of others.

Increasingly, however, our federal policy of regulations has another premise. Namely, that none of us can be trusted with freedom, and therefore none of us are entitled to the freedoms which were once commonplace. In other words, we are all treated, at the very least, like children.

Is this morally sound? It might be possible some time in the near future to achieve some very radical controls over all of us. Cars may be made so that we can never exceed the speed limit. Cigarettes and liquor can be totally abolished. A serious tax or heavy penalty can scare us out of being overweight. We may all be required to do conservation work, pick up street trash, made too afraid by radical penalties to risk sexual and other sins, and so on and on. Will we be morally stronger or morally weaker?

The fact is that as state regulations increase, we become morally weaker. It is basic to Biblical faith that moral strength comes from *inner* regulations, not outer ones. Our inner regulations are governed by our faith, character, and our religious convictions. The more we rely on outer regulations, the less we depend on inner regulations, the faith which makes them possible, and the freedom which gives them growth.

To distrust freedom is to distrust growth. To distrust freedom is to trust in statist controls rather than in God as the source of morality. When we try to make people good by statist regulations, we are declaring that they must remain permanently as children, that the state can produce a better moral life than freedom under God, and that the state knows best. This, I submit, is a very dangerous belief.

★ *eight* ★

DOES THE SUPREME COURT KNOW BEST?

NOT TOO LONG ago, the U.S. Supreme Court ruled nine to zero that the federal government may compel the Old Order Amish to violate their religious beliefs for "the common good." These Amish had objected to paying the Social Security taxes, but Chief Justice Warren Burger held that Social Security is a common good, and the Amish must pay it.

I was immediately reminded of the fact that the Soviet Union believes and maintains that it is the freest, happiest, and best nation on earth, but it keeps armed guards all along its borders to keep people from escaping all that happiness. If the Soviet Union were as good as it claims to be, the problem along its borders would be to keep people out. In the United States, our problem is illegal aliens pouring in, and they now number millions. The Soviet Union has the reverse problem.

We have here an obvious fact, but we refuse to learn from it. Social Security is nearly bankrupt, thanks to Washington's usual incompetence. Federal employees want no part of it. If Social Security were as great a common good as Warren Burger pronounces it to be, it would be no problem getting people to sign up for it. However, a rapidly growing number of people want out of it. Burger is talking the same kind of sense as the Soviet leaders; he calls a thing good, but he erects a fence to keep unhappy people in. We may soon see, if the press gives it any attention, some people going to jail out of religious conviction rather than into the Social Security fenced camp.

The plain fact is that the same money invested in a private insurance or pension plan would yield more returns than does Social Security.

Moreover, if private companies managed things as badly as does Social Security, they would be taken to court by the federal government.

We have for years made fun of the claims of the Soviet Union. No one needs guards, after all, to keep people in a paradise or inside a good thing. Then why are we threatening the Amish with jail if they refuse to go into Social Security?

The Amish have their faults, like all of us, but their virtues are also very noteworthy. They are a hardworking, law-abiding, and godly people. They are not a drain on the taxpayers at large. They take care of their own, do not have a criminal element, and are faithful to their beliefs.

Something wrong is going on in a country when the Amish are hauled into court, when Christian schools are persecuted, and when very fine children are arrested for delinquency because they attend Christian schools. From the earliest days of the Soviet Union, it has been the best element which has been persecuted — Christians, university professors, writers, farmers, and other like persons who should be regarded as assets to a nation. The U.S. Supreme Court, with its Amish case, has placed us on the same course of action.

This is the same court that overturned the death penalty of a young man who killed a highway patrolmen who stopped his car. The court ruled that the young man's troubled upbringing should have been taken into consideration by the judge who sentenced him. Thus, the Supreme Court did not respect the Christian faith of the Amish, but it did show concern over a murderer's home background. More than that murderer, the U.S. Supreme Court is something to be afraid of.

★ *nine* ★

IS EDUCATION FOR OR AGAINST BARBARISM?

The Key Reporter of the Phi Beta Kappa Society (Winter 1981–1982) recently carried an interesting article by Edgar F. Shannon Jr., commonwealth professor of English at the University of Virginia. The subject of Shannon's study is "Education: The Leaven of American Life." Professor Shannon has some good things to say and places some very needed emphasis on quality in education. Essentially, Shannon wants a restoration of character and emphasis on the liberal arts curriculum and the humanities. However, one sentence in Shannon's address stands out because it summarizes a common opinion. He states, "Education is what raises a society from barbarism to civilization."

Is this true? More than a few men have called attention to the role of education in creating the new barbarism of Mussolini's fascism, Hitler's Nazism, and Russian Marxism. Instead of raising those societies out of barbarism, education has been used to create it.

Education, obviously, can be put to a variety of uses. Just as some drugs can heal us and others kill us, so too education can be constructive or destructive in a society depending on who controls it and the nature of the educational curriculum.

One interesting fact, which may be a coincidence, but again, it may be a causal factor, is that federal entrance into education has seen a decline of quality go with it. During the 1950s and the early 1960s, academic achievement tests were showing a steady improvement. In 1965, the Elementary and Secondary Education Act was passed by Congress; we now have a Department of Education on the federal level. Since 1965, scores on Scholastic Aptitude Tests (and other tests) have fallen. Federal involvement in education would appear to be costly of two things: first, of quality and achievement in schools, and second, of money. We are paying more and more taxes to get less and less educational results.

Moreover, education is *not* necessarily what raises a society from barbarism to civilization. Some of my teacher friends have some distressing horror stories to tell of the rule of the new barbarism in our state schools. One able teacher told me that nowadays the restraints are mainly on the teachers, not on the pupils.

Furthermore, education is essentially a religious discipline; it is the communication of the values, learning, and achievements of a culture to its children. We are obviously not communicating sound moral values. The same is true of learning. With test scores dropping, even with lower testing standards, learning has been sacrificed. Certainly, we are not teaching any knowledge or respect for the achievements of our American society and culture.

Ideally, education should be good and constructive. Practically, it can be like a wife or husband: a marvelous joy if good, and a living nightmare if bad.

What we need to advance our society is not simply education as such, but good education—strong in communicating moral values, learning, and a respect for the achievements of our civilization. A good education is important to freedom, and a bad education destructive of it.

★ *ten* ★

ARE CRIMINALS AFRAID OF THE LAW?

ST. PAUL, IN Romans 13, makes a very important point which we dare not forget. The purpose of civil government, he says, is to be a terror to evildoers, not to the moral and godly people within that state. This is a basic premise which it is important for us to understand, and yet a very obvious one.

It is the criminal who should be afraid of the power of the state, not the law-abiding man. However, what we are seeing here and all over the world, in varying degrees, is a reversal of that fact. An authority on the subject, who has studied records from North America and Europe, says that only one to three out of a hundred crimes see a solution *and* conviction. Crime has become on the whole, a big and safe business.

On the other hand, the law-abiding citizen is in trouble with the law to an increasing degree. A few million are regularly audited by the IRS. These people have tried to make out their returns honestly, but too often they are treated like criminals. How true this is, I cannot say, but I get reports from all over the country that some police departments are told to give more traffic tickets to raise more revenue. If you improve your home, you get taxed for it, and so on and on.

More and more people want no contact with any branch of the state or federal governments because they find it an ugly experience and come away feeling like victims. Clearly, our situation is dramatically better than that of many other countries. The differences are very real. However, the plain fact is that too many citizens resent or are fearful of contacts with city, county, state, and federal agencies. They are afraid not only of the rising criminal element, but of the very agencies of state which are supposed to protect or serve them.

St. Paul said that civil government should be a terror to evildoers. It does not appear to be that today. One police officer told me of arresting the same hoodlum over a fifteen-year period, a man with a record of over thirty arrests and some convictions. Usually, the hoodlum left laughing before the officer had finished his paperwork.

If a civil government is a terror *not* to evildoers, but to the law-abiding, then it has lost its main reason for existence. Such a civil government has then become a self-serving power. It collects taxes to support itself, grow bigger and richer, and to increase its power and control over us.

Thus, St. Paul's definition is a very simple and basic one. Who is afraid to be out on the streets in your city—you or the hoodlums? Who is worried about going off and leaving the house unoccupied—you or the hoodlums?

When a society sees its people living in uncertainty and fear, not with security and thanksgiving, it is time to recognize that its civil government is in need of a radical reorientation of purpose.

★ *eleven* ★

WILL WISHING OR LEGISLATING MAKE IT SO?

I LEARNED OF some very successful counseling workshops that teach class members how to get rich by wishing for things. By paying $75 a day (or up to several hundred), you are taught how to wish for and get a new Continental or Mercedes Benz, the house of your dreams, or whatever else your heart desires.

These workshops are apparently very successful in attracting students, some of whom claim great results. The basic premise of these classes is that wishing—positive and informed wishing—can give us what we want.

Now, what do we do with groups like that? Some state officials seem to believe that licensure and controls are the answer. However, given the results of licensing psychiatrists and psychologists, the licensure route is not very promising. What licensure controls is a required educational background; it is by no means an assurance of moral integrity and professional competence. We are too often given a false sense of security by such licensing, as though the framed certificates on the wall have any relationship to integrity and character.

Well, what else can we do? The simple answer is, we can and should (in most cases) do nothing. If a serious problem develops, such as a financial fraud, we have enough laws to cover these cases.

There is, however, no way in the world that we can legislate foolishness out of the heart of man. What we can do by attempting to suppress every possibility of fraud is to eliminate freedom, and to destroy freedom is too high a price to pay.

Freedom involves your right and mine to be foolish, to make a mistake, to lose money through stupidity, and to pay the price of gullibility. We may or may not learn by our experience, but growth requires the freedom to make mistakes. No child learns to walk without first falling again and again. Without freedom, in other words, there is no growth.

I think it is ridiculous to pay $800 to learn how to wish. I already do too much wishing, and I do *not* believe that wishing makes it so. Working might. I have some possibility of getting my dream house or my dream car *if* there is some sense to my wishing and some work behind it.

The whole premise of licensure and control is that state supervision insures quality. If this were true, then we should find the highest quality and performance in the licensing agency of the city, county, state, or federal government. However, it is precisely in these controlling agencies that we usually find the poorest performance, the lowest quality work, and the lack of character which is so basic to integrity and performance.

Today, however, we have agencies and boards to license and control almost everything. There are hundreds, if not more, state and federal agencies to control almost everyone and everything except theater popcorn poppers, and maybe some states or cities have such boards. The licensing mania has become so bad that almost every occupation wants a certificate to hang on the wall stating that John Doe is a certified feather-plucker.

Well, it is now time for me to go to pick up a new dog license, my driver's license renewal, and a burning permit. I am glad, however, that my wedding anniversary, which is coming soon, will not require me to renew my marriage license, or is somebody at the state capitol planning to stick me with an annual renewal fee?

★ *twelve* ★

DO WE NEED A LICENSE TO DIE?

IT IS NOT as easy to die these days as it once was. I can remember when dying time meant that family and friends stopped by to say their farewells. On the day of the funeral, friends came from miles around, and everybody brought food for a big potluck banquet. Enough was left over to keep the family from having to cook for days after. It was also a big reunion. At the cemetery, some folks would show me their own gravesites and headstones with everything chiseled in except their death date. Dying was easy then.

What happens now? Well, all kinds of certificates have to be filed, and they cost money. State and federal taxes on the house, farm, or business can tie up a family for almost a year, and they also very often wipe them out financially. It's getting so bad that almost nobody can afford to die these days.

But this is not all. One law, which is catching on in state after state, requires that an autopsy be performed on the deceased if he or she had not been to a doctor within three weeks prior to death. Think of the implications of that. If you and I or anyone else is old or ailing, we must see a doctor, every month approximately, whether it does any good or not, or else an autopsy must be performed when we die.

This means a tidy and steady income for the doctor or else an income, then, for the coroner. Much of this is taken care of by Medicare, but, of course, our tax money pays for that.

Now, we have heard of ghoulish people who try to cash in on death. They come around, on reading a death notice, and claim that the deceased ordered something and then try to collect on it. Fortunately, there are not too many such people.

However, what can we say about our ghoulish federal and state governments which make death a time to gouge and rob widows and orphans? This subject is not a pleasant one, but I submit that any civil government that deliberately plans to make money out of the death and the grief of peoples has sunk as low as anyone can.

The Bible tells us over and over again that God regards the treatment of widows and orphans a key test as to the character of a people and a nation. God promises judgment on those who exploit widows and orphans. In other words, God sees it as thoroughly rotten and contemptible for a nation to use the time of bereavement and grief to rob and impoverish a people. We have, however, made this policy into law. One estate planner says that about 75 percent of all families are economically wiped out by the death of a husband or wife.

People sometimes talk about the high price of funerals, but such costs are a trifle compared to the toll exacted by the federal and by many state governments.

It *is* time we told the ghouls in Washington that we have had enough of this. The taxation of death is the ultimate insult a civil government can impose upon a people. It is a degrading and an evil tax. The rich can utilize some provisions of the law to protect themselves to a degree, but most of us are the victims of the Washington ghouls.

★ SERIES TEN ★

★ *one* ★

WHO IS CONGRESS WORKING FOR?

IN THE FIRST quarter of 1982, Congress did something that I should have commented on at once, but I decided to cool off first before I did. I can't say that my disposition on this matter has improved much, but here it is, anyway!

Congress voted itself a number of new benefits to increase its take-home pay. Members of Congress can now deduct almost anything they feel is even vaguely related to their jobs from their income tax. According to *Human Events* (March 6, 1982, 8), members of Congress can now "take generous tax deductions for their food, housing, servants, laundry, home maintenance, utilities — you name it." Members of Congress already have the most generous expense allowances above and over their salaries. They have a dream pension plan to protect them from problems if they lose an election.

By means of this new law, members of Congress, simply by using these special deductions which apply only to them, can get a write-off of as much as $22,875 of their annual income, according to the *Washington Post*. Add to this the deduction of their mortgage interest payments, their property and other taxes, and their other deductions, and their total tax-free income goes even higher — much higher.

When Congress passed this measure, the jobless rate was increasing; some unions were signing new contracts at the same or lower wages to keep their jobs alive, and many corporations were close to bankruptcy. Congress, however, voted itself a very substantial backdoor pay raise. You and I must pay the bill.

At the same time, Congress was grumbling about a tax cut for the rest of us; in fact, more than a few members of Congress were calling for higher taxes. We heard statements about how you and I are getting away from the IRS with too much of our money because of supposed loopholes. I wonder what constipated idiot decided to call it a loophole if you and I get to keep some of our own hard-earned money, and these days it gets harder and harder to earn it.

Congress is supposed to represent "we the people of the United States." Instead, it represents itself, and we are treated like sheep to be sheared. Congress is supposed to provide for foreign and domestic defense against all our enemies, according to the Constitution, but we are in a bind now that the framers of the Constitution never dreamed of: we need protection from Congress.

I do not mean to imply that all members of Congress voted for the bill. A substantial minority voted against it, and these men deserve our respect. The point is that a congress should represent, under God, the people. It should be responsible to God and to man. If Congress gives itself special privileges which are withheld from the rest of us, then our form of civil government is weakened and a serious lack of representation exists.

A battle cry of the colonial era was, "no taxation without representation." If a member of Congress is immune to the tax laws which govern you and me, what kind of representation is that? He then ceases to be anyone who shares and understands my problems, and my freedom and my vote are seriously diminished. We need a Congress which is subject to the same tax laws as the rest of us.

★ *two* ★

IS LAW ENFORCEMENT ALWAYS GOOD?

SOMETIMES, WE TAXPAYERS get a break. In 1980, Donald Lambro, in *Fat City: How Washington Wastes Your Taxes*, listed one hundred federal agencies which have been wasting our money; this list, he made clear, was not complete. The main function of these agencies is to spend money and to provide bureaucratic jobs.

The good news is that one of these, created in 1968, died on April 15, 1982, after spending nearly $8 billion of our money. This agency was the Law Enforcement Assistance Administration. Like all such agencies, this one was given a good name designed to make criticism difficult. After all, who is against good law enforcement, or education, or wars against poverty, and so on? Usually, however, the better sounding the cause is, the worse the agency and its work. Freeloading prospers best under a noble name.

This was true of the Law Enforcement Assistance Administration. For example, over half a million dollars were spent on a program to promote physical fitness among police officers. One of the ideas this project came up with was, as Lambro reported it, a desire "to develop Dick Tracy-type wristwatches that would allow police officers to obtain a quick reading of their blood pressure, temperature, and pulse while on the go." With this kind of gadget, maybe an officer in hot pursuit could ask to be relieved on the ground that his blood pressure and pulse rate had gone up!

Another project, funded at $27,000, was a study to determine why convicts want to escape from prison. You and I could have given the

Law Enforcement Assistance Administration a bargain-basement opinion on that and saved the federal government some money. The point is, however, when an agency thinks up subjects like that, it means that it is straining to find ways to spend the appropriated money and to reward some sociologist with a grant.

Another strategy was financed to find out why people move out of neighborhoods where the crime rate is high. People who take pay for producing such so-called studies must now and then have some twinges of conscience, I hope, about what they are doing. Streetwalkers are at least honest about what they are.

Lambro said of the Law Enforcement Assistance Administration in 1980, "There are a number of things wrong with this program, not the least of which is that it has had a difficult time spending its money" (265). All kinds of silly subjects were studied in the name of law enforcement, delinquency programs, and other such noble-sounding causes. Perhaps Congress killed the agency because it ran out of excuses for spending.

Well, Lambro tells us that there are at least ninet-nine more such bureaus that he can document as useless and wasteful. Maybe Congress even created some new ones to replace this one. One thing is sure: Washington is spending more money than in 1980, when Lambro wrote, and the jobless rate in Washington, D.C., (the lowest probably in the U.S.) is certainly not made up of civil service people.

Meanwhile, it *is* good news that one useless agency is dead. We can hope that many more will be finished off next year, before taxes finish off the rest of us.

★ *three* ★

HOW MUCH OF YOU DOES THE FEDERAL GOVERNMENT OWN?

ONE OF THE interesting facts about the United States is the amount of land owned by the federal government. In Alaska, 90 percent of the state is federally owned; in Nevada, it is 87 percent; Utah, 65 percent; Idaho, 64 percent; Oregon, 52 percent; Arizona, 45 percent; California, 44 percent, and so on down the line. Supposedly, these lands are kept in trust for the people, but in reality private conservation groups and corporations have done and can do a better job of it.

But this is not all. We need to ask another question: how much of us do the federal, state, and local agencies of civil government own? About five to ten years ago, we were told that between 40 to 45 percent of our income went for direct and hidden taxes; some now place that estimate at 50 to 60 percent. Whichever figure is right, it constitutes a very big share of our income.

Slavery is defined as a property right in the labor of other men. If you own a slave, it means that he must work for you. Very obviously, through taxation the civil government now owns about half of us, and this means that we are half slaves, whatever else we may call ourselves.

When the federal government, more than a century ago, abolished slavery, it abolished only the private ownership of slaves, not public ownership. In fact, all over the world, slavery is more common than ever before. In the communist bloc, all the people are slaves of the state. In the democracies, we are half slaves and half free.

What we need is an emancipation proclamation from slavery to the modern state. You can be sure that neither Washington, D.C., nor the state house will issue any such charter of freedom on its own. Only if we, the people, compel them to do so will the various branches of civil government disgorge their powers over us.

We may think we belong to ourselves, our family, our church, or our community, but with every paycheck, we are reminded that we belong to Washington, D.C., and before we see our paycheck, Big Brother has put his bite on us.

The plain fact is that the modern state owns too much of us. Instead of being our servant, it has become our master, and we have been steadily stripped of our assets and our freedom. Very definitely, it is time for a change.

To gain that change, we must be changed. As Paul says, "[W]here the Spirit of the Lord is, there is liberty" (2 Cor. 3:17).

★ *four* ★

ARE WE OVER-LICENSED AND OVER-TICKETED?

A FRIEND OF mine, a retired Army colonel, has a son who is in deep trouble for exercising old-fashioned American enterprise and initiative. He is a young man just starting out in the working world, and jobs for photographers are scarce. He is, however, making a good living in spite of that. For this, he may land in jail.

This young man takes his camera and a pony to supermarket parking lots to take pictures of children on his pony. The pictures are good ones, and popular with young mothers.

His problem, however, is the police; he does not have a license. Because this young man works in a metropolitan area of many suburban cities, to get a license for his territory means getting eighty-two licenses to be safe. To take out and keep renewed eighty-two licenses would mean that only all the cities involved would come out ahead in his work.

People like this young man get worse treatment in court than most criminals. Two weeks ago, he received a heavy fine, was told by the judge that he was the worst kind of lawbreaker, and then assured of a year in the county jail if he were caught again.

If you are mugged or robbed, the criminal is likely to get probation. This young man is apparently doing something far worse: he is preventing the city from collecting taxes!

Supposing he were to get the eighty-two licenses, which he cannot afford to do. Would his pictures be any better? All that the licenses would mean is that the city government would get their cut. We call the Mafia bad for shaking down businessmen. How different are these licenses? Do they not constitute a shakedown racket and a money-raising scheme?

Now, I believe that traffic tickets to people who endanger life and property serve a good purpose. But many of you are reporting to me that, in your city, all kinds of technical violations of no consequence draw tickets, and that in at least one case, councilmen have asked for more ticketing in order to have more city income. I hope this is not true, but the very fact that more and more people believe that such things are true indicates a radical lack of trust in civil agencies.

The fact is that we are over-licensed and over-ticketed. It is precisely the law-abiding people of our country who are made the targets of shakedowns at every turn. We pay the taxes, we pay the licenses, and we pay the tickets, and we get less and less for our money.

Times are bad, and that young man with his camera and pony had the right idea, not welfare but a paying job. Over and over again, we Americans have *worked* our way out of tough problems created for us by bad politicians. Now we have a tougher battle because this time it takes a license to work! We are limiting freedom and independence, and in doing so we are limiting our future.

★ *five* ★

DO YOU LIKE TAXATION?

A NEWS ITEM (San Francisco *Chronicle*, February 21, 1982) states that the current government of Vietnam has a new tax. A fine is levied against the estate of anyone who commits suicide. The technical charge is "desertion."

The attitude of the Vietnam government is that it is the duty of the people to stay alive to pay taxes. Obviously, the Vietnam government is working hard to catch up with the rest of the world. There is hardly a corner of God's earth where men are not taxed every time they turn around!

Here in the United States, we give the parents of every newborn baby a tax deduction, not much but still something. After all, that baby, once he or she begins to work, will spend most of a lifetime paying taxes. Babies may be a joy to their parents, but they are a potential bonanza to the taxman!

We are taxed, our property is taxed, our income is taxed, our dog must be licensed, our gasoline is taxed, our food, clothing, and entertainment is taxed, and when we die our estate is taxed. No wonder someone remarked that the two surest things in life are death and taxes.

Now, let us grant that both death and *some* taxes may be a necessity. But why add insult to injury? Washington, D.C., tells us that our income tax payment system is one of "voluntary compliance" (*Inquiry*, April 26, 1982, 4). Do *you* know anyone who is paying his income tax voluntarily?

This is not all. The Sixteenth Amendment to the Constitution—the income tax amendment—has no restricting clause whatsoever. It gives the federal government the right to tax our income as it pleases, up to 100 percent if it chooses. This is not an impossibility. Some foreign governments have done so. By taxing incomes up to 120 percent, they have liquidated wealth and estates. Because, legally, all our income belongs to the federal government, what we are allowed to keep is called an exemption.

Remember, the Internal Revenue Service did not do this; Congress did, and you and I elect Congress. The fault, in other words, lies in us. We are electing men for the wrong reasons, and we are not responsible electors. We are getting more and more taxation because we are demanding more and more benefits from state and federal governments.

Any benefits we get we must pay for, individually or collectively, and collective payments are the most deadly when they fall due. As an individual, I know that I cannot buy myself more benefits than I can afford. As a citizen, I do not see the bills fall due; I can only see the inflation and the growing national debt. As a result, the collective payments due are ignored by most of us until too late.

If we do not control both personal and collective spending, we destroy both ourselves and our country. We need, therefore, to exercise controls on both our spending and on our nation's spending.

Remember, we are getting the taxes our representatives voted for, and *we* voted for them.

★ *six* ★

ARE WE RUNNING LOW ON IDEAS FOR SPENDING MONEY?

I WONDER SOMETIMES if our planners sit up thinking of ways to test our patience. Some of their projects are really amazing ones. The Community Development Program of the Department of Housing and Urban Development came up with a choice one.

Baltimore has a well-known "Block" — several blocks long — of strip joints, "adult" book stores or pornography shops, peep shows, and the like. A total of $338,000 is being spent in this area to make it more attractive to customers. The pavement is being cut at various points to make tree planting possible, and wheelchair cuts have also been made in the curbs. Apparently someone has decided that it is discrimination to make it difficult for the physically disabled to visit their porno shop! The owner of one strip joint says, however, according to *Human Events* (May 22, 1982, 2), "What's really needed is sexier broads. Ya think Washington can help there?"

Perhaps I am unkind and am doing our bureaucrats an injustice. Maybe what we need is more concern for despised or neglected forms of American life. Let's help them by suggesting better means of spending money. Why not park benches on skid row so that our unfortunate people there can have something beside the pavement to sleep on? Or is that too practical and worthwhile a suggestion?

Why not a national museum, somewhere close to the Department of Housing and Urban Development, of old-fashioned "Chic Sales," or outhouses, which are becoming a fast-disappearing form of Americana? Has HUD no concern for our American past?

For some of us old enough to remember the days between World Wars I and II, one of the most common aspects of American rural life was the farm mule. I don't understand why our Washington politicians do not erect a national monument to the mule. They have a lot in common: both are stubborn in resisting orders, and both are impotent and sterile.

Perhaps I am too hard on politicians. After all, Will Rogers said that he never met a man he didn't like. However, Will Rogers never spent too much time in Washington, D.C. We Americans have a good sense of humor. This is the reason why we can live with our politicians in Washington, D.C.

Perhaps it is a mistake to poke fun at Washington. I am reminded of a story told years and years ago by Mississippi Congressman John Allen. A Confederate cavalry colonel was leading his regiment in a gallant retreat with the Yankees in hot pursuit. Some of the Confederates were turning now and then to fire at the Yankees. The colonel then gave this command: "Boys, stop that shooting; it just makes 'em madder."

★ *seven* ★

ARE WE BECOMING A POSTAGE STAMP REPUBLIC?

WHEN I WAS a boy, I learned a great deal about politics from my stamp collection. In those days, the total number of stamps issued by all the strong nations were very, very few. A collection of all the world's stamps (except the most valuable) could fit into one large album covering all stamps ever issued to 1940. Now almost that many are issued in two or three years.

In those days, many countries were known to us as "postage stamp republics." They were known as very shaky nations, politically and economically, and not likely to have a stable administration. Every few years, a new dictator would take over these "postage stamp republics." Two things especially marked these countries, and every boy could spot them in his stamp album.

First, the "postage stamp republics" issued new stamps all the time. Whereas the strong countries rarely changed their stamps, these weaker nations issued new ones several times a year. The main market for these issues was the stamp dealer and collector—cheap stamps for the unwary buyer. Sometimes, more stamps were sold to collectors than to users.

Second, these "postage stamp republics" had very obviously unstable economies. Not only were they constantly issuing new stamps, but the postal rates kept rising. Inflation as a fact of economic life was plainly confessed on every new postage stamp. The strong nations then had an unchanging postal cost; the weak, unstable, and inflationary countries had a fluctuating postal rate.

Thus, as a boy, I learned not only geography and history, but a great deal about politics and economics from my stamp collection.

It is a rather sad knowledge now because I can see that the United States has now become a "postage stamp republic." Every so many days, a new stamp, or a sheet of different stamps, is issued. These are issued to make money, because Washington knows that a few million Americans who save stamps will buy and never use these new stamps. The result is a considerable profit to the postal service, one of the few areas where it comes out ahead.

Moreover, our stamps also reflect inflation. In 1981, we saw an unprecedented fact in American history. We had three different postal rates in one year, fifteen cents, eighteen cents, and twenty cents. We may see more dramatic rises in postal rates in the years just ahead.

"Postage stamp republics" have a poor track record in history. They are marked by political instability, inflation, and a loss of freedom. It is time we changed something besides our postal rates.

★ *eight* ★

DOES CRIME PAY?

A GREAT MANY people in California were very unhappy recently because a con man was released from prison after serving only three years of a nine-year sentence. This man robbed a number of people of $9 million by operating a supposed "investment business" which was actually an elaborate Ponzi scheme. The con man thus served three years or paid a year for each $3 million in profit. An attorney for some of the victims said of Boron, where the con man was incarcerated, "It's a country club, not a prison. They've got tennis courts, a lovely swimming pool and a very lovely exercise room. The prisoners live in dorm-style housing" (Los Angeles *Herald-Examiner*, May 17, 1982, A1, A5). Some of this con man's victims lost their savings and their homes. The con man lost three years of his time, and nothing more.

Clearly, this is not justice. Very obviously, crime paid very well for this man, as for many others. Prisons are no deterrent to crime even at their worst, and the growing crime rate is of concern to all of us. It is time, then, to reconsider what the Bible requires with respect to criminal offenses.

The basic premise of Biblical justice is restitution. Restitution places the penalty on the criminal, not on the victim. If a man steals $100, he must restore $100 plus a penalty of another $100. Depending on the kind of thing stolen, restitution can be up to fivefold, according to Exodus 22:1. If a man cannot make restitution, he must become a bondservant and, by compulsory labor, be in servitude until restitution is fully made. For capital offenses, capital punishment is required by the Bible. In this system, the criminal is penalized, not the victim. In some states and localities, we are seeing a return to the principle of restitution.

A recent case revealed that one particularly degenerate criminal, whose profits run into millions of dollars, has deposited these funds in foreign banks. Such a step makes retirement abroad easier after a brief spell in prison at the taxpayer's expense.

The courts never asked the con man, who robbed trusting people of $9 million, to repay anyone. As taxpayers, all of them helped to support in prison the man who destroyed them, and they know that he will now have a beautiful home to return to — plus a mansion in Hawaii.

Crime *does* pay. This is one reason why crime is a major growth "business." Big money is being made in crime. I doubt that Benjamin Franklin would say today that "Honesty is the best policy." Honesty is the only moral and godly way of life, but our laws and courts are hardly making it a good policy.

Any society in which crime pays is in deep, deep trouble.

★ *nine* ★

WHEN IS RAPE NOT RAPE?

THE *New York* magazine (February 15, 1982, 16) reported earlier this year on a case of truly blinded justice. I have debated whether or not I should discuss it and finally have decided to report on it. Let me say, first of all, that not all judges by any means are like this one, but enough are to make it necessary to comment on it.

A young woman bank teller was robbed and raped by a hoodlum. She was held at knifepoint, her face covered by the rapist's jacket, and raped. It is reported that the New York judge asked the twenty-four-year-old young woman a single question: had she *seen* the rapist penetrate her? Since her face was covered, she said no. The criminal was acquitted of rape and first-degree robbery, but convicted only of nonviolent robbery and sexual abuse, both of which carry much lighter penalties.

Now, when is robbery *and* rape at knife point nonviolent? And where are we told that, if the victim's face is covered, rape becomes only sexual abuse?

The prosecutor rightly argued in court that if actual vision of the rape were necessary, no one could be prosecuted for raping a blind woman. The judge did not buy this argument. The district attorney's office felt that future rape prosecutions were all threatened, stating, "I've never heard of a woman watching penetration" in a rape case.

A source close to the judge said that the sexual abuse *might* have been with a dildo or hands. How often does that happen? And what is the difference? By positing hypothetical alternatives, almost any crime can be explained away.

All that can be said about such thinking is that, surely our muggers, thieves, and hoodlums are something to be afraid of, but so are many of our judges, right up to the very top. They seem to have as little knowledge of what justice is as many of our criminals and even less touch with reality. They are tender about the "rights" of criminals but not the rights of the victims.

Twice recently, I heard about men who were robbed of considerable sums of money. In one case, a man borrowed $20,000, and in another, a man owed $15,000. In both cases, they refused to pay. In both cases, they got away with it. When the two aggrieved parties looked into the legal costs, plus the court situation, they realized two things. *First,* it would cost them too much money and time to go to court. *Second,* even if they won, there was no assurance that they would be able to collect. In another case, a man went to court over $25,000, won a judgment, and still was not able to collect ten years later.

Justice and the law are parting company, and when they do, freedom is in trouble.

★ *ten* ★

ARE WE ROBBING WIDOWS?

WHEN IS YOUR property not your property? The answer to that question is, any time the federal and state governments choose to claim, tie up, or regulate your property, and they feel free to do so.

The *Farm Journal* (April 1982, 10) cited the case of a Missouri farm wife whose husband died. It was harvest time, but she could not use the farm machinery to proceed with harvesting. For her to have done so was held to be illegal, since the machinery was in her husband's name and tied up in the estate. To all her griefs and cares of widowhood there was now added another. She had to hire men and machines for the harvest.

I know that lawyers can give me long reasons why this was so by citing laws, cases, and precedents. The fact remains that the whole thing stinks. We are robbing widows. Our lawmakers seem to feel that widows are chickens to be plucked, not human beings. I wonder how state and federal legislators can look at the estate, death, and inheritance taxes and regulations they have passed and still look in the mirror without throwing up.

A woman can work alongside her husband to develop a farm or a business. She can be as much a part of it as her husband and sometimes more so. However, unless they have seen a lawyer and prepared for death, she is likely to see the taxman rob her of much that she spent years working for. Even seeing a lawyer is not enough. The laws are changed almost every year, so that a good legal provision of last year may be no safeguard this year.

Isn't anyone ashamed or angry about all this? Are we living in a society where the state and federal governments are so much at war with us that we must retain a lawyer to protect ourselves?

Our Washington politicians scream every time there is talk of a tax cut about the harm it will do to the poor. Has it never occurred to them that maybe taxes are making us all poor? Does it never bother them that they pass laws aimed at robbing widows?

We have several organizations of senior citizens in this country. Why are they not doing more to protect widows and survivors? Death is a sufficiently sad time without being made more so by acts of Congress.

It is high time we told our state and federal representatives to show more consideration for widows and orphans. We have many ugly taxes on the books, but perhaps none of them half so bad as those which tax death. Something is seriously wrong with a society which tolerates such a tax.

★ *eleven* ★

DO YOU WANT A VEGETARIAN WORLD?

ONE OF THE amazing facts about our time is that so many people are determined to control the rest of us and to compel us to live exactly as they do.

We have an animal rights movement today which is determined to protect all meat animals and assert their rights for them. Before you write this movement off as too far out to be worth talking about, let me tell you that it is holding well-attended regional planning conferences. In early summer, the "animal rights" movement was able to get Representative Ronald Mottl, an Ohio Democrat, to introduce a bill to study the question of animal rights and husbandry practices. A substantial number of letters requesting action on the bill reached the House Agricultural Subcommittee.

Alex Hershaft, a leader in the animal rights movement — and a vegetarian — defined the aim of the movement as the training and mobilizing of people to effect social change. He said, "The animal rights movement is a natural extension of other movements . . .civil rights, antiwar sentiment." He charged that "cows, calves, chickens, turkeys are raised under inhumane conditions on factory farms," and expressed as a goal the increase of vegetarianism.

At one conference, an attendee declared, "A nonviolent world has its roots in a nonviolent diet." In other words, world peace will come through world vegetarianism. If this were true, India, with its vegetarianism, should have a history of peace, which is hardly the case.

More important, what we have here is an effort to move towards regulations and controls which would coerce us all into vegetarianism. The procedure is, *first,* to create a national opinion that animal raising and slaughtering processes are cruel and disgraceful and should therefore be controlled. *Second,* the controls would lead to higher prices on meat to push more and more of us into involuntary vegetarianism. *Third,* in the name of animal rights, the next step may then be to ban the killing of food animals. Perhaps then we may get a vegetable rights movement, and we would all be on a diet of hot air.

I *am* for the freedom of these people to express their opinions and to convert others to vegetarianism. I am *not* in favor of their coercive tactics. Moreover, when freedom is used foolishly, it is then cheapened and begins to wane. Freedom requires responsibility to survive, not foolishness.

★ SERIES ELEVEN ★

★ *one* ★

ARE WE USING LANGUAGE TO CONFUSE OURSELVES?

TOO OFTEN IN our time, the terms we use to organize our thinking are created by statist agencies and serve to mislead us. One such set of terms created by the Internal Revenue Service is "profit" versus "nonprofit." Profit-making activities are taxed; nonprofit enterprises and agencies are not. People have come to classify activities in terms of these two terms, as though they described reality instead of a statist-categorization of taxation.

Would it not be much more realistic to classify things without reference to the IRS? How useful would these terms be, if the IRS were to disappear in the next decade? After all, they have reference only to tax status.

I submit that the terms "productive" versus "nonproductive" are much more useful. Churches, schools, and libraries are "nonprofit," but they are at the same time among the most productive agencies civilization has ever known. To eliminate them would be to eliminate civilization. Civil government is emphatically nonprofit; often it is not productive of too much good, but can be productive of social order when kept within its limits. The family is a nonprofit community, but it is, most emphatically, a productive agency. Its decay is the decay of society and civilization.

Because we have emphasized the profit versus nonprofit perspective, we have tended to falsify our view of life. In every area — intellectual, industrial, and personal—we have downgraded the productive man in favor of the profiting man. Production has thus been displaced by administration; the visible symbols of profitable power in church, university, state, and business have gained ascendancy over the productive mind and hand.

Religiously speaking, this means that form has become more important than substance and pragmatism has replaced theology. When we look at the world through categories governed by the IRS, we have beggared ourselves intellectually, and we have allowed the taxman rather than the Lord God to frame our thinking.

We need to remind ourselves of St. Paul's words:

> Study to shew thyself approved unto God, a workman that needeth not to be ashamed, rightly dividing the word of truth. (2 Tim. 2:15)

★ *two* ★

ARE WE REGULATING OURSELVES INTO TYRANNY?

READING THE NEWSPAPER is sometimes like reading one's own obituary. The news tells us that our country is committing suicide and, to make sure it succeeds, is trying several brands of poison: inflation, lawlessness, drugs, poor education, and more. High on the list of killer practices is overregulation.

As I was looking over a couple of months worth of clippings and articles, I found this one which I had saved (though not because I liked it):

> Trouble is brewing in University Park, Texas, a placid little island of affluence where city officials propose to allow building inspectors to enter homes to enforce a rigid repair code . . .
>
> The sixteen-page code proposal says, among other things, that homeowners can be fined up to $200 a day for weeds in the lawn, cracks in the stairway, or unsound chimneys . . .
>
> The proposal also authorizes building inspectors to initiate their own complaints and enter homes at any time to enforce the code.
>
> "I'm worried about this," said college professor Stephen Guisinger. "What's to stop the city from coming back and saying we can't smoke in our homes?"[1]

Weeds in the lawn are a nuisance, and its no pleasure to be reminded of them by your wife! But the idea of a citation and a fine by a city

1 *San Diego Union,* July 22, 1982, cited in *Inquiry,* September 1982, 2.

inspector is another matter. I may not like the way my neighbor keeps his place, but if I have the right to control him by law, then a neighbor with a place better than mine can legislate against me. If we start fining people for weeds on the lawn, why not fines for driving a dirty car — or too old a car? If we can be fined for having a house which does not suit the city inspector because of cracks on the stairs or in the paint, perhaps the next stop is to tell us that we ourselves are unfit for public viewing because we are overweight, wrinkled, bald, or what have you.

The whole philosophy of such regulations leads to tyranny and to a dictator-state. In a regulated state, everyone is keeping an eye on other people's business, and not their own.

Regulations governing our lawn's weeds may give us neater neighborhoods, but freedom is a high price to pay for weed-free lawns.

★ *three* ★

DO WE HAVE A NEW KIND OF PREJUDICE?

EARLIER THIS YEAR, the U.S. Court of Appeals for the Second Circuit in New York gave special privileges to the Communist Party. Whereas Republicans and Democrats who give more than $50 to a campaign must have a report filed by their party giving their name, address, and the amount of their donation, the Communist Party was given a privileged status in that no such donor reports are required of it (*National Review*, June 25, 1982, 736).

Now, up to a point, we can understand the court's apparent reasoning. No one ordinarily gets into trouble for contributing to a Republican or a Democratic campaign. It is possible that contributions to the Communist Party, if made public, could cause problems for the donor. But is this in fact the case? When and how often has a man suffered for giving to the Communist Party? I hear more often of problems connected with giving to United Way. Some people like to apportion their gifts directly to their preferred causes, and because many offices and stores want 100 percent giving, trouble ensues for the independent holdout. The point is that if we make an unpopular stand, we should be prepared to face problems because of it.

Our problem today is that we are trying by law to counteract problems of prejudice by reverse discrimination. Criminals have at times, perhaps, had to face a bias in court; now the bias is against the victims of crime. The essence of justice, as the Bible makes clear, is that there be no respecting of persons whether they be rich or poor, or anything else. We are now showing by law an emphatic respect for persons, and thus we are saying that favoritism to certain groups must have priority over justice.

We thus have a new kind of prejudice. Justice is suffering as a consequence. A juror in one lawsuit told me that the jury knew that the suit to collect a gigantic sum from a big company was a fraud, but $100,000 was granted because, they reasoned, "It's a rich company, and the insurance policy will cover it." Such thinking means the end of justice and the triumph of prejudice.

★ *four* ★

IS FEDERAL AID DESTROYING AMERICA?

I HAD A visit from a friend who has an all too common problem. He lives in hill country on a minor county road. There is only light traffic over that road, mostly by people who live there and some by people going through to fish or hunt in higher country.

The county has decided to widen the road considerably and make a highway out of it. My friend has two and a half acres; he will lose one acre to the highway, and about three-fourths of an acre will be rendered useless.

Some of the residents did more than a little investigating and found that the only authenticated need on that road was that an old, very narrow bridge be widened. At a board of supervisors meeting, they asked that the construction be limited to widening the bridge and that their homes and land be left untouched. The supervisor who answered them agreed that the only need was a wider bridge, but said, "We can only qualify for a federal grant for this road-widening project." In the process, the bridge will be widened, but all of us will pay for an unneeded and costly road project.

Incidents like this are commonplace all over the United States. All too many federal grants in aid are an invitation to unnecessary and costly projects. In the process, all of us are overtaxed, local officials are seduced into new and costly projects, and we are pushed further into national bankruptcy. Moreover, the bankruptcy we are drifting into is both moral and financial.

I said that my friend's problem is not an unusual one. Everywhere I go, I find people with like difficulties. If you knew the truth about many of the public works projects in your own neighborhood, you would find similar examples of unnecessary work and spending.

Is federal aid destroying America? Not exactly. For a people to be ready to go along with such useless and wasteful projects means that there is already something morally wrong with them. The federal government is simply aiding an already corrupt political system to increase the scope of their corruption. It's a racket in which all hands are guilty of cooperating.

Meanwhile, there are casualties: the financial stability of the country and the moral foundations of freedom.

★ *five* ★

CAN CRIME-STOPPING BE DANGEROUS?

A RECENT ISSUE of *Science Digest* carried a very important article by Richard Conniff entitled, "21st Century Crime Stoppers." (*Science Digest* 90, no. 8, August 1962, 60–65). The article deals with research into the prediction of crime. All of us are to some degree, involved in the prediction of criminal or abnormal behavior. We look at some of the neighborhood youth and predict that some of them will come to no good end. Sometimes we are right. Sometimes we are very, very wrong.

Now, however, we have scientists who believe that testing of various kinds will enable men in a generation or so, accurately and clearly to single out the criminal in advance, long before he has committed any crime, and even estimate how many crimes a year that person will commit. It is proposed by some that such people be jailed or executed in advance of any such behavior.

American Civil Liberties Union lawyer David Landau has protested against this kind of thinking, stating, "Almost all social-science studies show that you cannot predict the future criminality with any accuracy. There's also a constitutional objection. You're talking about punishing people for crimes they haven't committed."

There is another important objection — the religious one. Basic to Biblical faith is the doctrine of responsibility before the law for actual acts, not possible ones. The law must deal with actions to be just. Moreover, a person of eighteen may show every indication of becoming a criminal but later change. Perhaps the most vicious young hoodlum of eighteen I ever knew, from whom no one expected any good, was converted soon thereafter, went to college, and became a prominent university professor!

There are better ways of crime-stopping than jailing or executing potential criminals. We need to begin dealing with the actual ones. Besides, what if many of us who are innocent of any crime flunk the tests of these social scientists? Or what if these tests reflect political overtones, and those of us who are critical of the powers that be are found to be potential criminals? This kind of crime-stopping is not only dangerous, but is itself criminal.

★ *six* ★

ARE TECHNICALITIES DESTROYING JUSTICE?

THERE WAS A time not too many years ago when minor technical errors in the transcript of a trial were not considered consequential. Appeals were based on substantive errors, not minor nor technical ones. In recent years, however, this has changed dramatically; as a result, the law has become a legal game and not the means of justice.

Charles Peters, editor-in-chief of the *Washington Monthly* (October 1982, 4ff.), recently cited some examples of this game of law. In New York, an appellate court overturned the burglary conviction of a man with a record of twenty-one arrests and ten convictions. The man had been seen leaving the burglarized apartment carrying a television set. Two police officers were the witnesses. The defendant claimed that he had not even seen a television set until the officers approached him. The jury convicted him, and the appellate court agreed that the man was guilty, saying, "This evidence was certainly sufficient for a jury to convict appellant of the crime of burglary." However, because the prosecutor called the arrested man a liar during the trial, the court freed him. So much for the substantive question of guilt and innocence.

In another case, a New York dentist was convicted of sexually abusing a patient. The dentist admitted his guilt. The evidence was more than sufficient because he had been filmed in the act by a camera installed in the ceiling of his office. He was so aggressive that the woman investigator who posed as a patient had to be rescued at the last minute by detectives. The dentist admitted his guilt, but the conviction was thrown out by the judge because the warrant authorizing the camera had expired seven days before the camera was installed. However, the camera evidence was not even used in court because the dentist had pleaded guilty.

Is it any wonder that more and more people are cynical about legal justice? The courts have less and less to do with right and wrong and more and more to do with the game of law. The kinds of men who are appointed judges are increasingly contemptuous of the moral standards of God and man, and they regard criticism as somehow a sin against their sacred person.

Unless our courts again concentrate on and are governed by a doctrine of right and wrong — a belief in the *necessity* for justice — freedom and justice will both disappear.

★ *seven* ★

WHO GETS THE BENEFITS THESE DAYS?

RECENTLY (AUGUST 1982), *California Magazine* carried an excellent report on "The Burglar Cops of Hollywood." The Los Angeles Police Department caught some men in the Hollywood division breaking and entering stores to rob them. Several officers had developed a profitable sideline in stealing.

Two incidents followed which tell us how vulnerable and foolish our system of protection for workers can be. One of the bad cops involved was caught carrying cash and merchandise out of a store. He was taken to headquarters for a lengthy interrogation. Because he was on duty when arrested, he asked for and (in terms of the rules) was paid overtime for the hours of interrogation.

But this was not all. One of the officers allegedly involved in the break-ins and burglaries apparently found the experience of arrest traumatic. His doctor claims that the experience has created problems for the suspected officer, and that he is therefore entitled to a disability pension.

I wish incidents like this were a rarity, but they are not. Our laws and regulations seem to favor the persons out to exploit the system. For example, Charles Peters reports in the *Washington Monthly* (October 1982) that, in a sex discrimination case, the woman plaintiff was awarded $100,000 but her lawyers were awarded $2 million by the federal judge. I submit that this woman suffered more discrimination in court than she ever did before she went to court.

In the past generation, we have had many pieces of social legislation passed to provide a host of benefits. Many people resent any criticism of such legislation. My answer to all such is simply this: If you believe the food-stamp program is a good one, then you should lead the movement to rid the program of abuses, otherwise public disgust and protest will kill the program. If you believe that overtime pay and disability benefits are necessary, then work overtime to clean up the abuses before angry people destroy these benefits. If a program is designed to meet needs, yet becomes a means to help exploiters, in time no one will tolerate it.

★ *eight* ★

IS MEXICO'S PROBLEM AMERICA'S PROBLEM ALSO?

I BELIEVE THAT 1982 will be remembered as the year when the international bankers' chickens came home to roost as vultures. The United States, West Germany, and one or two other countries have for some time lent money to weak nations with little thought for our future. At the same time, private banks were also lending billions with no thought for our economic security and future.

Mexico now has an $80 billion debt; its economy is collapsing, inflation is severe, and the country cannot repay its loans. But Mexico is not alone. Argentina and Poland are in the same plight, and twenty-four other nations are joining their ranks.

To avoid a technical default, the banks are delaying the due-date on principle and interest payments, but failure to pay is still a form of default.

We are involved in all this, because the insecurity, weakness, or failure of our banks affects us greatly. Moreover, banks which have made heavy loans to weak and unstable nations who cannot repay them cannot then make loans to American businessmen, farmers, or buyers. In more ways than this, these bad loans abroad are going to have very serious consequences for the American economy.

What has been happening in Mexico throughout 1982 may be a hint of what will happen to all nations and economies around the world. Debt living will finally destroy an individual or a nation. Debt is a form of burning up our future by high living today. For some fifty years, we have been on a debt binge, and we have burned up much of our future. Salvaging America's tomorrow will not be easy. It will require a return to a sounder concept of economics than has prevailed over recent generations.

Debt living can be compared to burning up one's house to keep warm today, even though tomorrow one will be colder sitting in the ruins and ashes. In fact, it can be said that debt living has become the most popular means of national suicide in one country after another around the world.

Solomon was right: debt is a form of slavery. It is also the death of freedom.

★ *nine* ★

DONE ANY NAGGING LATELY?

ONE OF THE things which delights me is the study of words and their origins. One such interesting word is *nag*, as in, "my wife or my husband nags me." The word comes from Scandinavia, and it means to gnaw, bite, or burrow. It has an interesting history.

In the Middle Ages (and in many areas still), thatched roofs were commonplace. A roof could be a combination of boards, dirt, and straw. Such a roof became an easy nesting place for rats, as did the walls also. In fact, we know now that the plague was transmitted by means of these rats. People who lived in such housing were most susceptible to the plague, whereas those who lived in stone houses contracted it less often. At any rate, people who lived in simple housing had an unwelcome sound all night long: the rats gnawing away at their roofs and walls. The sound was irritating, unpleasant, and continual; it could not be turned off.

As a result, people began to use the word *nag* also for any talk they could not turn off, like a wife's complaint or demands or a husband's criticisms. Solomon said, "It is better to dwell in the wilderness, than with a contentious and an angry woman" (Prov. 21:19). With all the women he had, Solomon was an expert on nagging.

However, it would be unfair to say that all nagging is bad. Sometimes we need nagging to get to work that needs to be done. Samuel Adams nagged colonial Americans with his message of freedom until we became a free people. In fact, effective politics involves the art of nagging. Nothing has ever succeeded in politics on the first try. What has always been required is a dedicated and persistent group that nags at the powers that be until they wake up to the issue.

Our problem is that most of us have left this political nagging to others, and then we complain about the results. It is time we all started nagging our state and federal representatives; courteously, of course, but persistently. We need to tell them that this country is long overdue for a new birth of freedom. Freedom is worth fighting for, and it is also worth nagging and voting for.

★ *ten* ★

DOES BIONIC MAN HAVE A FUTURE?

ONE OF THE problems of our time is the unreasoning worship of science. We too often assume that anything science produces has to be better than what God did.

One television show of recent years featured a bionic man, another a bionic woman. The reality of such a person is with most of us, in part, and it is none too good. If you wear a pacemaker to keep your heart going, you are probably glad to be alive, but the pacemaker can never be as good as a healthy, natural heart. If you wear glasses, you are to that extent a bionic person, but two healthy, strong eyes of your own are far better.

The point is that the equipment God gave us is far better if we take care of it.

Take another example. Test-tube babies are highly touted as an amazing scientific advance. A more realistic view leaves us with grounds to rethink the matter. The press most readily reports successes in this area, not failures. About 95 percent of all test-tube babies die some time during the process. But this is not all. The work of Steptoe and Edwards showed an abnormality pregnancy rate of 50 percent. This puts a somewhat different light on test-tube babies. Apart from the moral issues involved, the normal process of conception and birth is dramatically superior.

A great deal of money is poured into a variety of experiments with life and birth, but the growing scientific establishment has a vested interest in giving us a favorable report on their work. In all of this, there are very serious moral issues.

There is also the simple fact that the results of scientific efforts do not give us something better than God created, but at best a crutch. Two great bionic achievements are eyeglasses and pacemakers, while another is the crutch for broken legs. These are good and useful things, but they are no substitute for good eyes, a sound heart, and sound bones. When people give us the idea that bionic man can be better, they are conning us, and our life and freedom may be at stake.

★ SERIES TWELVE ★

★ *one* ★

ARE THE COURTS AN ENEMY TO JUSTICE?

FOR MORE AND more people, the courts are a major roadblock to justice. The criminal seems to do better in the courts than the victim, and the whole judicial process is a costly drain on the taxpayer. The Supreme Court seems to be a place where folly, not justice, reigns supreme.

We can understand why this is so if we take a look at a key figure in twentieth-century American law. Oliver Wendell Holmes Jr. (1841–1935) was an associate justice of the Supreme Court of Massachusetts in 1882, and chief justice of that court from 1899 to 1902. From there, he went in 1902 to the U.S. Supreme Court, serving until 1932 for thirty very influential years.

The relativism and cynicism of Holmes can be summed up by his famous statement: "I am not here to do justice. I am here to play the game according to the rules." For Holmes, justice as something absolute and true did not exist; the law, for him, simply reflected the will of the majority of the people. This Holmesean attitude was summed up by a prominent criminal lawyer in these words: "What the hell is justice?"

This is our problem. A belief in justice is dropping out of our courts, our law schools, and our legislatures. The law is no longer the instrument of justice but the will of the people. If 51 percent of the voters are evil, then of necessity the law is evil.

Of course, the answer to this made by many is that there is no such thing as good and evil. An American philosopher, Walter Kaufmann, called for a social order beyond guilt and justice. For him, the ideas of guilt and justice were simply hangovers from the belief in God and should be abandoned.

If the law is only a game, as Holmes said, it is a very expensive game played with human lives. For those of us who pay the price as the victims of injustice, it is infuriating to hear justice reduced to a game where court officials and lawyers play with our lives and professions. The law and the courts as a game are destructive of both freedom and justice.

★ *two* ★

ARE WE SUFFERING FROM A NEW BIGOTRY?

A CASE IN a southern California court attracted a little attention far outside the borders of Los Angeles and Orange counties.

In April 1982, a destitute couple placed their natural child, a girl, with county-chosen foster parents in Pomona. The mother of the child was sick, and she was talked into allowing the child to be given to foster parents, who were fostering two other children. The child was placed in a home on April 22. There was no visitation in that home by a social welfare worker. The twenty-one-month old girl was sodomized by the foster father and died because of this sexual abuse on October 4, 1982.

Before going any further, it is necessary to say that there are many fine foster parents. I have encountered more than a few of them. Moreover, welfare workers are commonly overloaded with casework, and visitation sometimes gets neglected.

What concerns me is something more. As I travel back and forth across the country, I am encountering a serious problem. More than a few areas are rejecting very superior couples who are eager to be foster parents for a very ugly reason: the hopeful foster parents-to-be are devout Christians. This does not appear on the records. The statement is made orally, usually to the foster mother-to-be.

What we are seeing is a bigotry on the part of humanistic caseworkers against a responsible and moral element in our communities — the evangelical Christian. Is it any wonder, then, that we have sickening disasters from time to time, such as befell a little Monique Ann in Pomona?

What can we say for a country which rejects devout and godly people as foster parents? I am *not* saying that this is a rule across the country, but I am saying that it is happening, and it is an ugly sign of the times. Bigotry has many faces. This is one of them.

★ *three* ★

WHO GETS HURT BY BUDGET CUTS?

AS I TRAVEL back and forth across the United States, I find one dependable note in the television news whenever a state or federal budget is up for consideration. We are told that the budget cuts will hurt the poor and the aged, and we are shown some people who are going to suffer if the budget is cut. Now, these stories may be true, but the statistics tell us that the budgets are increasing, and the cuts are usually in the amount of the proposed increases.

This is not all. We are not told why some of our overgrown bureaucracies are not cut, nor why our legislators do not cut their own expenditures.

The next time we have budget talks, I would like to see interviews with the kind of people I know and recognize. One man tells me, "I am out of work, and they are raising my property tax." Another says, "I have had only few days of work in three months, but the Internal Revenue Service is claiming I owe them $400 from a year ago, and they may seize my pick-up truck." One woman in her eighties is upset because the IRS claims that she owes them $100.

The real news out there is that millions are finding taxation oppressive and confiscatory. The major burden for many is big government. When Proposition 13 was on the California ballot, the argument against it was that police and fire protection would be cut if the measure passed; none of this proved to be true. The same argument was used in other states. Nothing was said about cutting down on our bureaucracies.

I submit that we are getting the same ploy with respect to budget cuts. The poor and the handicapped are told that they will get the axe, but the legislators never axe the useless and overstaffed agencies.

The idea seems to be to lay a guilt trip on everyone who wants lower taxes, to make them feel like hard-hearted Simon Legrees.

Is it too much to expect honesty about budgets?

★ *four* ★

ARE WE OVERPOLLUTED AND OVERPOPULATED?

A FEW YEARS ago, I wrote a book entitled *The Myth of Over-Population.* It was a delight, therefore, to find a more thorough study of the subject: Dr. Julian L. Simon's *The Ultimate Resource.*

Dr. Simon documents the fact that we are not running out of farmland or food. Because of increased production, much farmland is returning to forests, wildlife areas, and recreational use. The world's food production is growing faster than the population. We are not running out of any natural resources, and, in fact, our known reserves are increasing dramatically. Instead of a diminishing energy supply, we have more and cheaper energy ahead of us in the future. Pollution has been decreasing steadily for some years, and population growth is not the reason for pollution. Population density does not create biological nor psychological problems. The standard of living improves wherever population increases. Immigration is beneficial, and illegal aliens actually pay in more by taxes than they ever receive as welfare, and so on and on.

Dr. Simon not only documents his case, but offers to wager $10,000 that raw materials will not be scarcer in the future than they are now.

Dr. Simon states that he once believed the myths of overpopulation, dwindling natural resources, and so on. However, when he investigated the subject thoroughly, he found the reverse to be true.

The cry of overpopulation and pollution is not new. It goes back at least to Plato. Plato's answer to this idea was a controlled and planned society. Today, those who propagate the myth have a like solution: *their* planning and controls. The myth has built into it the convenient answer of statist control to solve the supposed problem. The result is the death of freedom.

★ *five* ★

HOW BAD IS POLLUTION?

I REPORTED ON the data concerning pollution in the United States in the days of the horse and buggy. I called attention to the millions of tons of manure which then filled American cities, the germs they bred, and the pollution they created.

Now I have some data on London in 1890. In those days, London and all cities had a constant aroma of ripe horse manure, which floated as dust in the air in the summer, and became a wet, sloppy mess in wet weather.

The reports of the day indicate that foot traffic was difficult. The manure soup splashed up on everyone as the carriages went by. The Strand area usually had an eighteen-inch mess of liquid slop, which made for messy travel in an open buggy and major problems for pedestrians.

This was not all. The noise pollution of horses was far greater than that of automobiles. The pounding of innumerable horseshoes — four to a horse — on the pavement was far more noisy than the sound of a motor. Moreover, wagon and buggy wheels did not have rubber tires and were themselves noisy and often squeaky. Add to that the neighing of the horses, the shouts and curses of their drivers, and the crack of whips, and you have bedlam.

Of course, if you want real pollution, go back 200 years to 1783. Cities then often had no sewers. American cities had an outhouse smell to them. In many cities in Europe, chamber pots were emptied into the streets from upstairs windows. This made for very serious pollution for the unwary pedestrian underneath the window.

Now, by comparison, we don't know what pollution is today! This does not mean that we should not continue to improve our situation, but it does mean that the cause of truth and freedom has not been served by misrepresenting the problem. Technology has not increased but has rather decreased pollution.

★ *six* ★

WHO IS TAKING CARE OF THE POOR?

ONE OF THE greatest tools used by the Soviet Union against us is misinformation. However, the Marxists are not alone in this, although they are the experts at it. State and federal agencies regularly give out press releases which are mild but real forms of misinformation. Too often, the press, instead of digging for data, is content to use handouts. The net result is a distorted picture.

Let me illustrate. The greatest welfare agency in the United States is not the federal government but the American family. More sick members, elderly parents, and relatives are cared for by the family than any other agency. Add to that the millions of children from kindergarten through high school in Christian schools financed by the parents, and you have an impressive fact. More parents pay more for college and university education than does any other agency. The family is history's most impressive and most successful institution for coping with human problems.

A second great agency is the church. Every city has a homeless floating population and many transients. Protestant and Catholic missions to the inner city do far more than most people realize to alleviate such distresses, and they do this with too little help, very economically, and often with real hostilities from local welfare agencies.

This is not all. Some of the richest and most powerful evangelical businessmen in the United States have an organization, called Strategies to Eliminate Poverty (STEP), to work to alleviate poverty. This racially mixed group is already active in some inner-city areas. Their purpose is to provide relief and to make new persons out of the poor to enable them to get ahead. They already have some impressive results.

Freedom is better served if we have more information on what the free sector is accomplishing.

★ *seven* ★

DO WE HAVE A DYNASTY OF WEALTH IN THE UNITED STATES?

THERE IS A common impression that most great wealth in the United States is inherited wealth. The fact is that the world of economics is a world of change. Very few of the big corporations of 1910 are still with us, and this means that the fortunes those corporations created are disappearing. Of the 150 richest Americans, twenty-six are women, most of whom inherited their wealth, but more than a hundred of the wealthiest men made their money on their own (*Review of the News*, September 29, 1982, 35).

This is not all. At present, new fortunes are being created by younger men in microelectronics. They will, in a few years, displace the 150, whose fortunes will often be divided and dwindle.

At the same time, new forms of energy and new developments in technology promise to appear in the next twenty years. Each of these will create new fortunes among a new crop of younger men.

This has been the American story. In a changing economy, the center of wealth continually shifts and changes hands. The great men of wealth of the horse and buggy days have now a family of great wealth in only a few cases. In fact, the wealthier the family and the corporation, very often the less likely it is to be innovative and receptive to change. The result is that the United States remains the land of opportunity and the place where the poor can rise to the top.

The truth is that most of us are better off than our parents were. Our children will be still more prosperous. The standard of living for most of us has improved and will improve still more.

This does not mean that we have a problem-free society, nor that we can be smug and self-satisfied. It does mean that a free society is a mobile one in which a man can better himself. The defense of freedom is thus a concern to all of us.

★ *eight* ★

WHAT IS WRONG WITH DEFICIT SPENDING?

UNDER CONSIDERATION TODAY is another constitutional amendment banning deficit spending. The amendment would require that federal spending equal revenues and that federal expenditures cannot grow at a rate greater than the gross national product.

The proposed amendment has been attacked by one of America's major newspapers as trivializing the Constitution.

The purpose of the proposed amendment is to extend the Bill of Rights to cover our economic rights and prevent the federal government from passing confiscatory taxes. There is also the matter of common sense. How long can you and I, as individuals, survive economically if we run up a huge deficit every year?

The federal government is well beyond a trillion dollars in debt and close to bankruptcy. Social Security is in serious trouble, and so are other programs. At the same time, Congress has passed the highest budgets in history, and we are seeing also our largest deficits. Common sense should tell us that sooner or later a day of reckoning will come for all reckless debtors, whether they be persons or nations.

There is, however, another aspect to this issue: the moral one. Debt living, whether in persons or nations, is a product of bad morality, and it creates an even lower moral level as a consequence. Historically, times of inflation have also been eras of lowered moral expectations, high crime, family conflicts, and social disintegration. What we buy when we incur debt is a growing decay in the quality of life.

Deficit spending is thus economically wrong and also morally wrong. It is also a serious political error in that it creates economic inflation and, with it, social unrest which leads to a distrust of political processes. Remember, it was massive inflation and political disillusionment which preceded the French Revolution, the Russian Revolution, and the rise of Adolf Hitler. Any nation which indulges in sustained deficit spending first bankrupts and destroys its most stable citizens, and then it destroys itself.

Thus, an amendment to forbid deficit spending by the federal government is a necessary step towards the survival of our form of government and of freedom.

★ *nine* ★

WHO GETS HURT WITH TRADE CONTROLS?

IN 1982, AN interesting protest took place in Japan, and the United States was the target. Japan's twelve top petrochemical companies are in trouble. They are each losing about $4 million a month, and they demanded that the Japanese government act at once to stop the flood of cheap, foreign, chemical imports. Those cheap imports were coming from the United States, and American prices are half those of Japanese companies (*Inquiry*, October 1982, 2).

This sounds very familiar, does it not? Some American companies complain about the cheap Japanese imports, and some Japanese companies complain about cheap American imports. Both sides say that the other country is costing them jobs. What is the answer to this dilemma?

There is another factor that needs consideration before we answer that question: the consumer. If you and I, or the man in Japan, can get something from abroad at half the price, we save money, and it gives us more funds to spend on something else. This means that, besides the American and Japanese corporations *and* their workers, our own personal economic well-being is at stake. If Japan taxes American imports heavily to make them closer in price to Japanese products, and if we similarly tax Japanese goods, the consumer is the loser.

Economic freedom in international trade benefits the consumers, who are in the majority over any one or more industries. If our automobile industry cannot compete with foreign imports, all the protection we give it will only postpone the day of reckoning. On top of that, we need to realize that the United States has usually done best with new products and new inventions. By the time other countries start producing them economically, we are up ahead in a newer technology.

It is a mistake to think, therefore, that foreign goods are a threat to us. They usually free us from one kind of production to a newer one. Some very able experts predict that we are on the verge of the greatest of industrial revolutions. It is happening in "Silicon Valley" in California and will change the face of American industry and vastly improve the standard of living.

Economic freedom promises us some dramatic changes and improvements in our material advantages.

★ *ten* ★

SHOULD LIFE BE BETTER AT THE TOP?

A NEWS ITEM sitting on my desk has been irritating me. One Washington, D.C., commission head, in the latter part of 1982, decided to have his office and his agency's chief counsel's office remodeled and redecorated at a cost of $85,000 (*Inquiry*, October 1982, 2).

Now, $85,000 is more than most of us paid for our whole house. As taxpayers, we have to pay for better housing and better offices for our bureaucrats. The agency head remarked, "The place looks shabby the way it is." Does your office or your house look shabby the way it is? Are you paying the boys in Washington to live better or to govern better?

I would agree quite emphatically that people in superior positions should live better. The idea that an important executive should get no more than his lowliest employee is nonsense. It is a sound Biblical principle that a laborer is worthy of his hire; the more responsible and important his work, the better should the rewards thereof be.

There are, however, limits to all this. Too often, our top men in state and federal governments live in palatial circumstances, with every kind of service and convenience provided at our expense. There is a very real distinction between a deserved compensation and exploitation.

Increasingly, it appears that, at some levels, the compensation of civil officers has made the transition from a just and due reward for services rendered to exploitation. Then we the taxpayers become the exploited. Life should be better at the top, but it should not be exploitative. Moreover, remember that we are paying all civil officials to govern better, not to live better.

Some people are entitled to special privileges because they render important and special services, but when those privileges become exploitative, a distance is created between the men at the top and the people.

That distance is growing, especially now, with both inflation and increasing unemployment. It is a very unhappy and foolish thing for federal officials to feel that large sums of money be spent to provide them with royal accommodations. In doing so, they bring to their office the contempt of the American people, and they tarnish the forms of freedom.

★ *eleven* ★

ARE WE A NATION OF BOOK BURNERS?

WE PERIODICALLY READ that some group or other is upset because a school board wants to keep certain books away from school children, and the impression is given that some people known as "the radical right" are involved in book-burning. How true is this?

Moral Majority, for one, is charged by some with book banning, but that group has never been involved in such activities, nor has Eagle Forum.

It is true that parents in many communities have objected to certain books because of their content and in the belief that those books are unfit for school libraries. It is also true that libraries and library journals recommend certain books and reject others, often because they are too conservative or too Christian. If we call the one censorship, we must also call the other the same.

The fact is that both sides want children to get the best perspective on life, and to cloud the issue with charges of book banning is to misrepresent facts. All the books in question can be bought by anyone at any bookstore. The Christian school will obviously avoid certain books as not worthwhile or as definitely bad. Similarly, the public school, being governed by a humanistic faith, will select books which conform to its perspective and reject others; this will, of course, offend some parents. The solution is not name-calling.

Basic to freedom is the fact of choice. If we deny freedom, we are denying choice. What these people who rail at the supposed book banning are really saying is that there can be no free choice for anyone except themselves. If I want the freedom to choose, I must also give that freedom to others.

True book banning would be the prohibition of publication; it would involve stopping a book before it is printed. In some countries, nothing can be published without a state permit. Any violation of that process is severely punished.

We have nothing even remotely resembling that in the United States — not yet, at any rate. It is a very grave disservice to freedom to misrepresent issues and to speak of the threat of censorship where no such threat exists.

★ *twelve* ★

WHO MAKES HISTORY?

AMERICAN U.N. AMBASSADOR Jeane Kirkpatrick, in her book *Dictatorship and Double Standards* (1982), wrote most tellingly of an illusion common to many of our professors, bureaucrats, statesmen, and politicians. This illusion is the idea that vague "social forces" shape events rather than people.

Ambassador Kirkpatrick cites evidences of this very dangerous myth. If social forces create events, then it becomes necessary for civil government to engineer those forces, which will create the desired results.

Such a belief, however, makes people the creatures of forces rather than God's creation. It also reduces man to a helpless piece of driftwood on an ocean of social forces. Such thinking is radically alien to our Biblical faith and heritage. Our civilization and our country are the products of men of faith and action who shaped events and set forces in motion rather than being shaped by them.

I submit that this belief that social forces shape events is a new religion, not sound sociology. I submit also that it is a very damaging faith. It produces pessimism and a sense of futility. It cuts the vital springs of human action and channels energy into self-defeating concepts.

History is not a product of vague social forces but very real peoples, who by faith embarked on brave ventures and made great steps forward. Behind every great age of advance in history, we find men of action vitalized by a powerful faith.

Forces do not exist in the abstract. A social force is the product of a people's faith and action. It has no existence in and of itself, and it cannot exist apart from a people's beliefs. Social scientists, in talking about such forces, have fallen into a naïve deification of their own ideas. History is a human product, not an abstraction's work. Not surprisingly, these scholars have converted history into social studies to strip events of their human source and to ascribe them to vague social forces.

Such a faith, however, denies man freedom and reduces him to a product of vague, nonexistent "entities" or forces.

★ SERIES THIRTEEN ★

★ *one* ★

ARE WE STILL THE HOPE OF THE OPPRESSED?

THERE WAS MORE than a little publicity given to the fact that a Chinese tennis player defected to the United States and was given political asylum.

From the early days of the United States, we have been known the world over as the land of the free and a sanctuary for political refugees fleeing from tyranny. The sad fact is that this is less and less true. We did accept the Chinese tennis player, but there are some 1,000 other Chinese seeking asylum, and we are in no hurry to grant it.

Some time ago, we returned to Soviet authorities a Russian seaman who jumped ship. Prominent defectors do get asylum usually, but all too many lesser ones are not accepted.

But this is not all. In the past, political refugees from all over the world were, as a rule, a major force in overthrowing tyrannies at home. Now we restrict their freedom activities. For example, the Cuban refugees in Florida would like to have the freedom to broadcast into Cuba, but we deny them that right. Thousands of Cubans have been sent by Castro into Africa without any desire on their part to go. Many thousands have been killed in Africa, and their families have not been told. The Cuban refugees would like to broadcast into Cuba the truth about the deaths in Africa. They have the names of their war dead, as well as data on what is happening in Cuba of which most Cubans are ignorant, and so on.

We are, however, denying them this freedom. Many believe that such honest broadcasting into Cuba could lead to the overthrow of Castro. Why do we oppose it?

We used to pride ourselves on being "the land of the free and the home of the brave." Freedom fighters from all over the world found sanctuary in the United States and worked from here to gain their objectives at home. While maintaining a proper diplomatic relationship with all nations, we kept an open door to their oppressed peoples and gave them freedom to work for freedom at home. This fact contributed much to our worldwide popularity for generations.

Now, step by step, we are abandoning that policy. We seem to be more concerned about peace with tyrants than with freedom for their oppressed peoples or for their refugees. Perhaps the reason for this is that, at the same time, we are allowing our own people less and less freedom.

After all, we cannot champion freedom abroad if we do not expand it here at home.

★ *two* ★

WHAT ARE WE FINANCING WITH FOREIGN AID?

FOREIGN AID MONEY from the U.S. federal government and foreign loans by U.S. banks now finance a worldwide network of operations hostile to American interests. It would be difficult for anyone to justify the vast sums given to the Soviet Union, to Red China, and to other Marxist countries as anything but financing our own destruction. Much of the Soviet Union's military technology is made possible by our money.

But this is not all. Many "Third World" countries receive American aid, and their use of these funds is rarely examined. For example, two of my staff associates recently spent about three weeks in Bangladesh. A major dam had been built there with American funds; there was nothing wrong with the dam itself, but before construction began, human sacrifices were offered to ensure the dam's success. One thousand Christians had been sacrificed in that instance. Again, my associates asked a U.S. official about the construction of Bangladesh army compounds in the hill country which were built with American aid. No American officer or official has made any inspection (least of all a surprise inspection) of them. The fact is that the Bangladesh army does occupy these compounds, but they also serve as concentration camps for the hill tribes. The ruling peoples of Bangladesh are Bengalis; the hill tribes are not of the same race, and hence, they are persecuted. Their farms are open to squatters, and the hill tribes must stay at night in army reserves.

Is this unusual? On the contrary, it is routine. Our funds are given away or loaned out without any real supervision or follow-up. If an American receives a federal or a bank loan, he is extensively investigated and supervised. If he or she receives welfare, there is a measure of follow-up by social workers; we may feel that this follow-up is inadequate and careless, but it is still far more than is ever done with foreign aid.

The fact is that we are financing evil all over the world. Our foreign aid and foreign loans would, in many cases, do far less harm if we simply took the money and burned it up. In the long run, it would cost us less, and it would do less damage.

Foreign aid has become a major cause of our worldwide political and economic crises, and it has been a means of financing tyranny and slavery. Foreign aid and loans finance the enemies of freedom and the agencies of human bondage. It is time to call a halt to this evil.

★ *three* ★

ARE YOU A PATRON OF THE ARTS?

VERY FEW OF us have the money to finance art works, and if we did have it, we would prefer to pay for what we believe is good art.

All of us, however, through our tax dollars, are very definitely patrons of the arts. The annual appropriation for the National Endowment of the Arts budget is being pushed closer and closer to the $150 million mark. These millions go to many things most of us would consider bad art and to much we would not at all call art. In recent years, such funds have been used to produce a film on making blue cornmeal bread, for producing a "Gay Sunshine Journal," to publish a feminist publication, to acquaint ex-criminals and ex-drug users with art, and much more.

Some of the funds go to strange causes. The National Conference of State Legislatures is a lobbying group, but it has received Arts funding. The same is true of the National Council on the Aging, also a lobbying group.

In Washington, D.C., one sponsor of an erotic art show received funding, and so on and on.

Of course, some in Congress will argue that $150 million is not much. If may not be much to Congress, but it is a great deal to the rest of us. Moreover, we have our growing deficit because grants of $150 million to many thousands of like causes add up to billions of wasted dollars and an economic crisis.

We are regularly told by state and federal officials that their budgets cannot be cut. What we are not told is of the thousands of foolish grants which are regularly made and need to be eliminated totally.

Our national deficit is becoming the national disaster. Taxes are increasing, and so too is the tax revolt, a dangerous fact in that it represents a growing vote of dissent and no confidence in our form of civil government. If Congress continues to spend money as usual, it will not only bankrupt the country but also destroy all confidence in our constitutional order. The end result of fiscal irresponsibility and inflation has all too often been a totalitarian regime.

Those who want subsidies for the arts should remember that such subsidies, which are always followed by controls, are the hallmark of every totalitarian state.

★ *four* ★

ARE WE AFRAID OF WORDS?

ONE OF OUR growing problems is our fear of words — of name-calling. All too many minority groups do outrageous things, and if criticized, cry racism. The same is true of many non-minority groups; they perpetrate all kinds of nonsense and evil, and when caught at it, charge their critics with being "against the people."

For example, in 1971, Sixties radicals demanded certain things of the federal government in the name of Indian rights. They received 643 acres of federal lands with buildings to set up a supposed university. The school established, D-Q University, has never met any of the necessary, elementary educational requirements. It has received at least $7 million in federal grants. Its chancellor has been Dennis Banks of the ultra-leftist American Rights Movement, and DQU has been allied with Marxist groups.

The federal requirements which were a part of the original grant of land and funds have never been met. Accreditation was required and has not been attained, nor a minimum student enrollment. The original 1971 agreement required the return of the property if the terms were not met. Not only has DQU failed to meet the terms, it has failed to maintain the property, and it has leased out the land illegally.

In spite of all this, the people of DQU are making all kinds of charges against the federal government and accusing it of attacking an American Indian and Chicano project.

To make matters worse, DQU is suing the federal government with the aid of the Native American Rights Fund, a National Support Center of the federally-funded Legal Services Corporation. As research director Michelle M. Rossi noted in *Eye on Bureaucracy* (March 1983), "The U.S. government is essentially financing a lawsuit against itself, in that NARF (the Native American Rights Funds) received approximately $205,000 in 1982." In other words, we financed this nonsense, and now we are financing both the attempt to dissolve it and to preserve it. Everyone gets consideration except the taxpayer.

Moreover, all such groups need to do to gain major media coverage is to charge bigotry and racism. It is time to stop fearing names and words before freedom is destroyed by our timidity and negligence.

★ *five* ★

ARE WE IN A BANKING CRISIS?

RECENTLY, CONGRESSMAN RON Paul of Texas reported on the international banking crisis. He called attention to the fact that the world debt is expanding steadily and rapidly. "Third World" and communist states owe Western nations and banks nearly $1 trillion. According to Congressman Paul:

> This debt must be liquidated and this can be done in only two ways: by countries defaulting or by the debt being paid off with inflated dollars. The former approach requires the bankers to suffer the consequences of their actions; the latter method forces the American people to bear the cost for bailing out the banks and the debtor countries. It would involve a massive intervention by the Federal Reserve and the destruction of our money through the continued depreciation of the U.S. dollar. The mechanism is already in place for a further expansion of money and credit, in order to sustain the system for a while longer. This means that long-term inflation will persist and get much worse. (Congressman Ron Paul, "The Banking Crisis," in *Freedom Report* 8, no. 3, March 1983, 1)

But this is not all. Other debts bring the worldwide debt total to an estimate of over $10 trillion, and the annual interest on that debt comes to over $1 trillion at the rate of an average 10 percent. This means that the world economy, as well as the world tax structures, have a major problem simply meeting interest payments, apart from any payment or principle.

More and more nations are increasingly unable to pay their debts. If you have a savings account, the money loaned out to dead-beat nations may be your money, and their failure to pay can endanger your bank and your deposits.

The evidence is clear that we do have a world banking crisis. Behind that crisis stands the ugly fact of debt. Since World War II, men and nations have gone into long-term, heavy debt as though tomorrow would never come. Now, as the economy falters, the burden of debt grows heavier and more oppressive.

The economic and banking crisis will not be solved by economic measures alone. We definitely do need a return to the gold standard and to sound banking practices. Both, however, presuppose a mentality opposed to long-term and ready debt.

A debt-ridden people are not a self-reliant and free people. Debt is a form of slavery, and, worst of all, a self-imposed slavery. Are we ready to be a free and a responsible people? Being debt-free is an important aspect of freedom.

★ *six* ★

ARE WE MISJUDGING OUR PRISON CONVICTS?

A MURDER TOOK place inside the Men's Central jail in Los Angeles, California: a young man of twenty-four, in prison for six months for petty theft and battery, was murdered because he refused to pay $5 a week to live. A prison gang was extorting money from other prisoners and beating into submission all who refused. This young man, having refused to pay, was beaten and kicked to death less than a month before his release date.

Fifteen street gang members were arrested for the murder. Two were eighteen years old, one was twenty-four, and the other thirteen gang members were between nineteen and twenty-three years of age. All were in prison on charges ranging from parole violation to murder.

The extortion racket was not unknown to the jailers. According to Deputy District Attorney Peter Berman, "Any (non-gang) member was to be charged $5 (a week) to live on the row, and if he didn't like it, he would be beaten up. The jailers would have to remove him and bring in another guy to be extorted." The fifteen gang members were arrested, but we can probably be sure that nothing will be done to the jailers, who are — in a sense — accessories to such extortionism.

This crime, of course, was only a brief glimpse into the cesspool life of prisons. Homosexual rape is routine in jails. Prison life is a monstrous evil, and yet prisons were originally started as reform institutions.

Our problem with prisons is that we begin and end with a false doctrine of man. Humanism holds that men are either naturally good or, at worst, morally neutral. The solution to criminal behavior then becomes rehabilitation, trying to change the prisoner's outlook and lifestyle.

I believe it is time to view criminals again as sinners, as men with an evil bent. To be under any illusion about the nature of criminals is to be more and more defenseless in dealing with them. When parents of young hoodlums and murderers tell us that their sons are really good boys at heart, we need to challenge that assumption. I am weary of reading about model boys suddenly going wrong, only to find out too often that they were manifesting their evil character long before, only to have their parents cover up for them. When such people cover up their son's evil, they only encourage him thereby to feel free to indulge his criminality all the more.

If we regard our criminals as unfortunate men and boys, we are misjudging them. If we treat criminals as people who are really good at heart, we are fools and suckers. The more respect and freedom we give to evil men and to criminals, the less freedom there will be for us to enjoy.

★ *seven* ★

WHO ARE THE DEBTORS IN AMERICA?

QUITE FREQUENTLY, NEWSMEN, politicians, and people generally talk about the huge burden of debt carried by the poor people of America. I have even heard a few speak of the need for some kind of moratorium on the payment of debts.

Thus far, such talk is not too commonplace, but before the situation gets any worse, it is important to get the facts straight. While it is true that debtors include all classes of people, it is not true that all classes of people are equally in debt. One of the most basic facts for us to grasp in this matter is that the poor have the fewest debts of all. A really poor man can rarely get a loan; he is generally considered a bad risk, and few lending agencies are ready to consider his application. The poor are poor. They are commonly hard up for money, but they are not often in debt, and if they are, then only for minor things.

The middle class will tend to have more debts than the lower class, but even here the debts are limited. They are primarily loans against houses and farms and also small businesses. Since the middle class tends also to be the savers, their debt picture on the average is not really a bleak one, although many do have serious problems.

When we come to the rich, we find a much higher ratio of debts. To illustrate, a couple owning a lovely home in a superior neighborhood had it on sale for over two years. None of the prospective buyers could get a bank loan until a much richer man, who could have paid cash for it, bought it with a bank loan. For a variety of reasons, including the tax break for interest payments plus the advantage of keeping a large amount of cash free for investment purposes, the buyer sought a loan, and the bank readily granted it. A sizable percentage of debtors are rich to begin with. They are the ones who can borrow money most easily.

This is not all. A vast amount of the public's debt has been contracted by corporations. These are the main debtors in America. Plant expansion, new branches, the purchase of subsidiary firms, and much, much more make corporations the major debtors in the non-statist sector.

I am not calling attention to this fact to make any conclusions. I am doing so because we cannot have a realistic awareness of the nature of our debt structure apart from this knowledge. At the same time, we need to remember the much more ominous debts of our cities, counties, states, and the federal government.

If debt is a form of slavery, as Solomon said, we are in trouble.

★ *eight* ★

CAN A HOLE IN THE GROUND BE PRODUCTIVE?

THROUGHOUT AMERICAN HISTORY, we have had an element in the population very much opposed to the Puritan work ethic. Instead of holding to useful work as the key to productivity and to prosperity, many have had a variety of "gimmicks" to suggest as an easy way to national wealth. More than a few have insisted that printing more money would create more wealth; instead, it creates inflation. Others have believed that prosperity would come and poverty disappear by means of the passing of laws; if this works, why not pass laws to abolish sin and death?

In 1874, Richard Schell, a Wall Street stock speculator, became a member of Congress. Schell had a solution for the economic problems of his day. He wanted the federal government to dig a canal from New York to San Francisco. This would have been quite a task, considering that in 1874 only horse-drawn earth-moving equipment existed to tunnel through the Rockies! Schell wanted greenbacks to be printed to finance the project.

More recently, in 1936, in *The General Theory of the Employment Interest and Money*, Keynes wrote, "To dig holes in the ground, paid for out of savings, will increase, not only employment, but the real national dividend of useful goods and services" (Rep. Ron Paul and Lewis Lehrman, *The Case for Gold* [Washington, D.C.: The Cato Institute, 1982] 95). Remember, since at least 1932, Keynes's theories have governed the Western world, the United States, and other nations as well.

As a result, we have had all kinds of nonproductive federal spending, the idea being that any such spending will automatically bring about prosperity, no matter how useless the cause. Because of Keynes's idea of prosperity through useless holes-in-the-ground projects, we have hundreds of federal agencies which exist merely to spend money.

If Keynes was right, then our farmers are foolish in wasting time and money planting crops which bad weather can destroy. Instead, it would be much safer simply to plow the ground and ask for a subsidy to do so. As a matter of fact, under the influence of Keynes, this is exactly what the federal government began to do some years ago. Farmers were paid for not planting anything. Remember, Keynes believed that digging useless holes in the ground would, in his own words, "increase, not only employment, but the real national dividend of useful goods and services." Our politicians believed him.

No wonder we are in trouble!

★ *nine* ★

SHOULD UNIVERSITIES GET PENTAGON FUNDS FOR RESEARCH?

EACH YEAR, THE Defense Department awards contracts to industry for research and for new technology. Such grants are necessary and proper as long as they are honestly granted to the bidders who can deliver the best weaponry at the lowest prices.

A lesser grant was to colleges and universities. The new contracts rose to $852 million for the fiscal year, essentially for research. During the Vietnam War era, such grants were a major concern to the student protestors, and more than a few riots and incidents resulted. Spring 1983 began with a student protest at Ann Arbor, Michigan, against the University of Michigan's defense contracts.

Before the matter goes further, it would be wise to examine the issue carefully. It is fitting and right for industry to get such contracts, and industrial research and development departments are the major sources of our modern technology in every field. Few people appreciate the extent to which industrial research produces the inventions, technologies, and advances of our era. Without industrial research, we would have very little technology and scientific advance.

In the development of technology, the role of the university is a very minor one. The university, where science is concerned, is more involved in *teaching* than in anything else. Moreover, its scientific concerns tend to be *theoretical*, not practical. As a result, the involvement of the universities in Defense Department grants or contracts is actually a minor matter. The 1982 contracts to industry totaled $116.7 billion, whereas those to colleges and universities came to $852 million. In other words, it is much less than 1 percent of the total. Obviously, the Pentagon does not see university research as important.

It is possible that such university grants are made partially towards funding those schools whose alumni are important in Congress and the bureaucracy. It is questionable whether the grants to universities are very productive. What good the universities do could probably be better done elsewhere. Education will be better served if the contracts go elsewhere. This is not because defense work is demeaning to science, but because the essential purpose of a college and university is and should be education. Whenever *any kind* of fat research contract is dangled before professors, teaching suffers and the professors profit. With some schools, the rationale is that a few students gain opportunities for more research, but the reality is that there are better options in industry, and teaching suffers when the university is involved in defense contracts.

We have too many universities greedy for such contracts. Education suffers as a consequence. To harm or depreciate teaching is not practical.

★ *ten* ★

IS OUR FEDERAL BUREAUCRACY OUT OF CONTROL?

U.S. News & World Report (April 4, 1983) carried an article entitled, "Washington's Red Tape Just Keeps Rolling Out." The article called attention to several important facts.

First, the federal government often loses our records, papers, and tax returns. We are not forgiven any delay in filing papers and tax returns, but the federal government can delay indefinitely in providing us with data we need, or our tax refund, without any penalty whatsoever. This is a one-sided relationship which leads to arrogance and corruption.

Second, federal regulations, tax forms, and instructions are written in an unintelligible gobbledygook. We have in the United States today thirty million illiterates and almost thirty million more who are functional illiterates. If Ph.D.'s have trouble understanding many of the federal regulations, laws, and instructions, how can the rest of the people understand them?

Third, the paperwork is continually increased. I received a form from one department which asked for *voluntary* compliance, with no penalties for failing to return it. As an agreeable man, I filled it out and returned it. As a result, I was sent a second and longer form with a letter telling me of the penalties for failing to comply. One way to get clobbered by Washington, it seems, is to be an agreeable and willing citizen.

Fourth, we can add that much, if not most, of this paperwork is useless, and it does nothing except to spend the taxpayer's money on useless projects. Useless information is not information but disinformation. It has a negative and harmful role.

As long as the bureaucracy is not trimmed, the people are. We pay the high cost of misgovernment and overregulation. As a result, inefficiency and corruption are increasing because the federal bureaucracy is too big to control *except* by some dramatic and ruthless cutting. At present, there is no such cutting in sight. In fact, bureaucracy is our major growth industry.

Every administration for decades has promised to cut back while increasing the power and scope of the bureaucracy. We are less and less governed by our elected officials and more and more by bureaucracies. We are increasingly getting a kind of government which cannot be called either a republic or a democracy but only a bureaucratic oligarchy. As this new regime develops, freedom wanes.

★ *eleven* ★

IS THERE A RETURN TO RELIGION?

MANY MAGAZINES AND commentators have written about a return to religion. Is this true? Is there evidence of a change in the United States?

First of all, we have had in the past half-century more than one return to religion which meant little or nothing. A return to faith involves more than joining a church or buying more religious books.

Second, a return to religion can be a product of social stress rather than a believing heart. I can recall in the 1940s hearing a returning soldier say that, under fire in a foxhole, he prayed; when he came back, he headed for a bar and a prostitute, and he laughed about his foxhole religion. Because of the economic problems today, more than a few people are ready to act religious who, with prosperity tomorrow, will forget the faith.

On the other hand, some of the statistics are quite interesting. The evangelical churches have gained members in the years from 1972 to 1982 and the modernistic churches have lost them. During those years, the Southern Baptists gained by 20 percent, the Assemblies of God by 62 percent, and the Seventh Day Adventists by 36 percent. The United Methodist Church lost 10 percent, the Episcopal Church lost 15 percent, and the United Presbyterian Church went down 21 percent (*U.S. News & World Report,* April 4, 1983, 37). In other words, the stronger the faith, the stronger the growth. Clearly, there is a return to and a growth of a more Biblical and evangelical faith. This means that it is more than a church growth, because many churches lost, but it represents instead a faith growth.

Even this, however, is not enough to ensure a lasting return to faith. Together with a faith growth, there is also an obedience growth. One telling evidence of this is the great increase every year in the growth of Christian schools. This indicates that parents take seriously their responsibilities under God. Another indication is the growth of various agencies to deal with problems of delinquency, drugs, family stress, and more from a Biblical perspective. Another evidence is the development of agencies to minister to poverty, unemployment, and crime from a Christian viewpoint. We can also add that major groups have been formed to call attention to the problems on the political scene, in the realm of economics, and more.

All this is promising. A valid and enduring return to the faith means that all of life is viewed in Biblical terms and in terms of a mandate from God. Such a renewal, if it continues, offers hopes of a new birth of freedom and self-government.

INDEX

D

E

J

K

L

M

N

O

W

Z

ABOUT THE AUTHOR

ROUSAS JOHN RUSHDOONY (1916–2001) was a well-known American scholar, writer, and author of over thirty books. He held B.A. and M.A. degrees from the University of California and received his theological training at the Pacific School of Religion. An ordained minister, he worked as a missionary among Paiute and Shoshone Indians as well as a pastor to two California chuches. He founded the Chalcedon Foundation, an educational organization devoted to research, publishing, and cogent communication of a distinctively Christian scholarship to the world-at-large. His writing in the *Chalcedon Report* and his numerous books spawned a generation of believers active in reconstructing the world to the glory of Jesus Christ. For the last twenty-six years of his life, he resided in Vallecito, California, where he engaged in research, lecturing, and assisting others in developing programs to put the Christian Faith into action.

THE MINISTRY OF CHALCEDON

CHALCEDON (KAL-SEE-DON) IS a Christian educational organization devoted exculsively to research, publishing, and cogent communication of a distinctly Christian scholarship to the world at large. It makes available a variety of services and programs, all geared to the needs of interested ministers, scholars, and laymen who understand the propositions that Jesus Christ speaks to the mind as well as the heart, and that His claims extend beyond the narrow confines of the various institutional churches. We exist in order to support the efforts of all orthodox denominations and churches. Chalcedon derives its name from the great ecclesiastical Council of Chalcedon (A.D. 451), which produced the crucial Christological definition: "Therefore, following the holy Fathers, we all with one accord teach men to acknowledge one and the same Son, our Lord Jesus Christ, at once complete in Godhead and complete in manhood, truly God and ruly man . . . ." This formula directly challenges every false claim of divinity by any human institution: state, church, cult, school, or human assembly. Christ alone is both God and man, the unique link between heaven and earth. All human power is therefore derivative: Christ alone can announce that, "All power is given unto me in heaven and in earth" (Matt. 28:18). Historically, the Chalcedonian creed is therefore the foundation of Western liberty, for it sets limits on all authoritarian human institutions by acknowledging the validity of the claims of the One who is the source of true human freedom (Gal. 5:1). The Chalcedon Foundation publishes books under its own name and that of Ross House Books. It produces a magazine, *Faith for All of Life*, and a newsletter, the *Chalcedon Report*, both bimonthly. All gifts to Chalcedon are tax deductable. For a complimentary trial subscription, or information on other book titles, please contact:

Chalcedon • Box 158 • Vallecito, CA 95251 USA
www.chalcedon.edu